W9-AYR-438

THE IMMACULATE DECEPTION

The Bush Crime Family Exposed

Russell S. Bowen

Copyright © 1991 by Russell S. Bowen

All rights reserved. Printed in the United States of America. No part of this book, either in part or in whole, may be reproduced, transmitted or utilized in any form or by any means, electronic, photographic or mechanical, including photocopying, recording, or by any information storage and retrieval system, without permission in writing from the Publisher, except for brief quotations embodied in literary articles and reviews.

For permissions, or serializations, condensations, adaptions, or for our catalog of other publications, write the Publisher at the address below.

Library of Congress Cataloging-in-Publication Data

Russell S. Bowen, 1924-
    The Immaculate Deception: The Bush Crime Family Exposed
    by Russell S. Bowen
      p.   cm.
    ISBN 0-922356-80-7

92-4441
CIP

Published by
AMERICA WEST PUBLISHERS
P.O. Box 2208
Carson City, NV 89702

Printed in the United States of America
10 9 8 7 6 5 4 3 2

Acknowledgment

The author would like to acknowledge and extend a special thanks to Grant McEwan for the immensely valuable research, ideas, and support he gave that were crucial in helping to make this book become a reality.

Contents

ABOUT THE AUTHOR

Russell S. Bowen

When the author graduated from Los Gatos Military Academy in California in 1942, he already had been in uniform for nearly a decade. He spent his whole childhood in military training, attaining the rank of captain at the Castle Heights Military Academy.

At the age of 17, he became an aviation cadet after passing the examination in Sacramento, California. Still only a teenager, he spent the war years flying P-38s, dueling German planes in Italy as a "Top Gun" fighter pilot. He was a highly decorated pilot with the famous 82nd Fighter Group which demonstrated their fearlessness, dedication and supreme skill by flying combat aircraft under murderous conditions.

Following a meeting with the Pope at the Vatican in 1945, Bowen, at 19, was offered the chance to join the secret team of OSS directed by General William "Wild Bill" Donovan. Bowen became an undercover agent, involved in a variety of secret missions.

Bowen was assigned in 1959 to visit Asunción, Paraguay, to familiarize himself with the traffic routes of drugs coming into the U. S. through Cuba. His information on routes passed on to U. S. Customs was described as "the most important piece of information" they had received.

In his military career and as a strict Catholic, Bowen had been trained to follow orders from his superiors without question. Forty-seven years as a mole and member of William Donovan's secret team "Super Spies," he received orders and reported directly to William Casey, William Pawley, and his brother in the Dominican Republic, John Knight. In 1958 and 1959 he reported to Batista's Secretary Villalon, the Argentine who became the right hand man for Reagan. Still supported by several intelligence patriots Bowen survived operation "Silver Star," his last role. That same deference to authority led Bowen to carry out an operation that cost him six and a half years in a federal prison in Springfield, MO. Bowen, an undercover agent in a cocaine smuggling scheme that he was trying to expose, took the fall after diverting a drug load to Sylvania, Georgia rather than following orders which required him to deliver it to Homestead, Florida.

Among his many awards and decorations for meritorious service is the Distinguished Service Medal. After World War II, he flew numerous emergency airlifts and rescue missions as a free-lance pilot. He served as a flight officer for such world figures as the United Nation's leader Dag Hammarsköld, the Shah of Iran, and Cuban leader Fulgencio Batista. Among many other citations, Bowen received a commendation in 1956 from U. S. Army Major General J. F. H. Seitz for bravery rescuing a wounded army captain in Iran. Bowen even regulated the flight altitude to make his patient comfortable. "In the opinion of my surgeon, these actions by Captain Bowen may have meant the difference between life and death," wrote Seitz.

Bowen regrets that in his youthful idealism and his desire to excel, he was misled by some American leaders who claimed to be the guardians of America. Instead, they were then and are now damaging the country. Acknowledging that in his zeal to expose wrongdoing, he himself committed illegal acts (under orders from his government), Bowen has dedicated his life to exposing our government's ineffective and counter-productive efforts to curb the drug trade. He labels that current effort under the misguided control of U.S. President George Bush "nothing more than a war of words." And he asks that readers of this book who have information about the U.S. Drug Trade contact him through the publisher.

Bowen is a retired Brigadier General in the U. S. Army. He lives in Florida.

INTRODUCTION

I Come Not To Praise Thee...

"When the president does it, that means it is not illegal."

Richard Nixon

*"When the commander-in-chief of a nation finds it neces-
sary to order employees of the government or agencies
of the government to do things that would technically
break the law, he has to be able to declare it legal for
them to do that."*

Ronald Reagan

"Read my lips. No New Taxes."

George Bush, candidate for President, 1988

It was not just another routine cable that George Bush
received on November 1, 1975, in Beijing, China. The public
image he presented was that of an ambassador boldly forming
U. S. policy towards his host country but the reality was that
media darling Secretary of State Henry Kissinger told fake
world statesman Bush exactly what to say and do.

This cable was not another routine instruction, however.
New U. S. President Gerald Ford, smarting from criticism of his
pardon to Watergate-beleaguered Richard Nixon, asked Bush to
head up the CIA. Acting upon his always strong opportunistic
motives, the tall, reedy-voiced Bush must have sensed this was

a chance to get back to the U. S. and to return to politics. He quickly consulted his wife, Barbara, and cabled his acceptance.

It might have sounded like a new development, to have a former ambassador and congressman head up the CIA — and it certainly was big news in the media — but there's evidence that Bush secretly had long been active in the CIA. Why was Bush selected? Speculation was that popularity-seeking President Ford's motive was mainly to get Bush away from political contention in the 1976 race which the President was facing.

By the end of January, Bush was confirmed by the U. S. Senate. He moved into the CIA's tree-shrouded, suburban-looking Langley, Virginia headquarters, office number 7D5607. It's an unattractive, L-shaped office with a square sitting area and a column incongruously placed in the middle. Room 7D5607 is a cramped alcove housing not much more than the director's desk. Picture windows overlook a panorama of the deep, verdant Virginia woods.

What Bush did here in this inconspicuous office was a metaphor for his entire career. He acted busy. He held a job. But his accomplishments were limited to self-serving initiatives. Those who knew him then say that if he was deferential and obsequiously loyal in previous jobs, he was downright obedient in his new role as chief spy for the U. S.

But none of this should come as any surprise.

Here's the public face George Herbert Walker Bush would undoubtedly like to see perpetuated: Courageous war hero, popular Yale Phi Beta Kappa graduate, successful businessman, devoted family man, old "China hand," deft U. N. diplomat, successful anti-drug czar, charming scion from an old-line American family and if that's not enough, the "Great Liberator" of Panama and Kuwait.

That's not the real face of the president.

It's only a mask.

Strip away that popular image and the American people have the face of a monumental hypocrite and consummate political opportunist. The face belongs to a man who never has to worry about his convictions because he does not have any. He has no principles. He has shown himself ready to make any deal at all with but one criterion — does it serve his own self advancement?

For example, in 1980 while opposing Ronald Reagan for the GOP presidential nomination Bush was pro-choice abortion. After losing to Reagan and signing on as his running mate, Bush converted to anti-abortion, Reagan's position, which he has maintained since to prevent fallout from the party's right wing. No one really knows his real position on this moral issue if, indeed, he has one.

Throughout his career, Bush has always seemed to be in or around major events of our times from say the Kennedy assassination to covert wars and economics initiatives. His proximity to these events supports the belief of some observers that he may have played a part in them.

At times, it is certain he had a role, often peripheral, often obscure and frequently denied — a mystery man darting in and out of calamitous events — and now, a presidency that is a voyage without purpose or direction and with only one goal: re-election.

The establishment press for the most part, has largely ignored the real Bush, who attained the highest office in this country despite a record of deceitful dealing. Peel away the mask and the real face of George Bush emerges as someone who:

- Was an abject failure as Drug Czar for the Reagan administration.
- Had a close relationship with a network of anti-Semites with Nazi and fascist affiliations.
- Had a widely documented connection with the 1980 "October Surprise," the group which sabotaged Jimmy Carter's efforts to have the Iranian hostages released.
- Had a role in trying to delay the Watergate investigation after Richard Nixon put him in charge of the Republican National Committee.

- Encouraged the CIA to go back to business as usual, including covert and dirty trick operations, when he took over in 1976 (giving him the dubious distinction of being the only U.S President who was also head of the CIA).
- Was a strong supporter for the secret 1986 arms shipments to Iran.
- Had a mysterious role in the Kennedy assassination.
- Helped General Motors to kill a "smog decree" and was instrumental in blocking environmental reforms.

The latter fact came out recently when the *New York Times* graded Bush. The headline in typical Bush fashion pointed out his record here was one of "contradictions," as it seems to be on most issues.

Illustrating once again how he will do and say virtually anything for self-advancement, Bush at one point supported and indeed applauded the Clean Air Act. However, that was before the election.

"But now, with a Presidential campaign in progress and the economy stubbornly sluggish, the law, the most comprehensive and expensive environmental statute ever enacted, is under attack with the administration, where business interests often seem to outweigh environmental issues," wrote the Times.

The story on the front page of the Times noted that while Bush has never been a strong environmentalist, he had in standard hypocritical fashion when he won the White House said he supported the popular American perception that our environment needed protection. But that's changed. Available evidence, the story pointed out, lends support to a reversal of policies pursued by Bush's predecessor.

Richard H. Meeker, president of the Association of Alternative Newsweeklies and publisher of Willamette Week in Portland, Maine, says that if the average American voter had been reading the alternate press's coverage during the last election, George Bush would never have won.

It appears, on paper at least, that Bush's entire life prepared him for the presidency. He served eight years as vice president. Prior to that, he was in the U.S. Congress and was a diplomat. His life might be described as serving the public.

But it was not the public he was serving. It was himself. Throughout his career, he's been adept at worming his way into the confidence of people who then find something for George to do. Unfortunately, these "something" type of jobs never get done when George takes them on. He's proven himself a failure at every position he's held. What is particularly troubling is that he is now at the helm of the free world, responsible for the future of America.

Perhaps Bush's failures should come as no surprise, however, because he has never been in touch with his fellow Americans. Even when the rest of the country was plunged into the Great Depression, Bush's family was living in a large, dark-shingled house with broad verandas on Grove Lane in the exclusive Deer Park section of Greenwich, Conn. The family's every whim was taken care of by four servants—three maids and a chauffeur.

It has become obvious that Bush's rise on the national stage that he has come to dominate has been almost directly proportional to the decline, if not degradation, of the American constitutional structure. The sheer magnitude of negative ramifications by Bush's possible return to the White House with a sham "mandate" has compelled the author to put aside a number of other crucial investigations to devote months of careful research to bring before the American people the true face of this man who would be dictator of U.S.A., Inc.

There is no end to the Bush deception machine. Much of what he and his public relations people present as accomplishments are often detrimental to most Americans while at the same time benefitting Bush himself.

There is, for example, the contrived spectacle of Bush's Operation Desert Storm against Iraq, that left its leader, Saddam Hussein, the President's partner in the oil business, safe and sound. Before this country is drawn into another pre-planned and choreographed mini-war with the likes of Iraq, Libya or North Korea, Americans deserve access to the hidden details and secret agendas of the main proponents.

Bush insisted in 1990 that "our quarrel is not with the people of Iraq." The point was to "liberate" Kuwait, a principality which, in the words of another presidential candidate, H. Ross Perot, "defines decadence." In that struggle, Bush likened his "real enemy," Hussein, to a modern-day Hitler.

That is an interesting comparison, right on target, in fact. Saddam had been boosted in his rise to the fourth largest military power in the world through secret contracts with Bush and his cronies in much the same way that the Fuhrer's Third Reich had been financed by George Bush's father, Prescott Bush and his friends, Henry Ford and others, more than a half century ago.

That's only part of the story. There's the travesty of Senate confirmation hearings for his nominee to the U.S. Supreme Court, Clarence Thomas. Washington Post writer David Broder said that move was planned more than a year before the nomination to mobilize Bush's conservative base and to drive a wedge into the Democratic coalition.

Broder said, "Such considerations may strike you as cynical. But they are a great deal more honest than President Bush's pretense that he searched the country for the best possible nominee and was surprised and delighted to find that it just happened to be a black conservative named Clarence Thomas."

There's more. How about Bush's much-touted role as America's chief drug cop in the Reagan Administration? He headed the South Florida Task Force and the National Narcotics Border Interdiction System in the mid-1980s that left everything to be desired.

A telling commentary was that his leadership of the task force was not renewed after he served one year on it. By the fall of 1986, soon after Bush had left his position there, Florida drug enforcement officials admitted that the amount of narcotics smuggled into the U. S. had skyrocketed. At the same time, the Government Accounting Office (GAO) reported that cocaine imports had doubled over the previous year.

The Bush-controlled U. S. Justice Department is generally regarded as a national disgrace for its foot-dragging in the investigation and prosecution of virtually any cases involving drugs. As the former Commissioner of U.S. Customs, William von Rabb, declared in disgust when he resigned in the summer of 1989:

"The war on drugs is a war of words." The only real battles, he said, are being fought against the minorities and downtrodden, while those in authority are protecting the government's monopoly in the trade.

The first impetus to begin this book came in 1976, as the nation was still reeling from the revelations of the Church Committee about the well-documented CIA misdeeds. Chilean diplomat Orlando Letelier and his assistant Ronni Moffitt were killed that year by a car bomb on Washington's Embassy Row. Why was CIA Director George Bush unwilling to aggressively pursue the killers, who were later discovered to be members of the Chilean secret police?

A few years later, 52 American hostages in Teheran were released within 20 minutes of President Reagan's inauguration. Was this the "good old boy network" of George Bush...again? Ironically, it was Bush who coined the term "October Surprise."

What is important about this book is the fact that had Americans known some of the facts that will be presented here, hopefully we might have avoided some of our mistakes.

The obscene spectacle of "Operation Just Cause," to name one example, could have been averted. That coldly calculated move pushed by the Bush administration removed Panama strongman Manual Noriega. Had the American people been aware of his three-decades-long association with the CIA, the civilian death toll from that operation — believed to be over 4,000 human beings — could have been averted.

In the same way, despite some efforts by American patriots, few in the U. S. in 1988 knew of the plan to assassinate CIA asset Noriega for his role in drug dealing.

Lt. Col. James "Bo" Gritz, Commander of Special Forces in Panama, revealed the attempt 12 years earlier to "remove this wart from the nose of a decent society." But that effort had been shelved by the ultimate insider, then-CIA Director George Bush, according to Gritz. All Americans suffered through the following years as tons of cocaine poured into our country, undeterred by Bush who essentially condoned a massive drug infestation that he might have prevented.

In typically hypocritical fashion, he privately thwarted a real effort at curbing the drug trade while publicly taking the stance that he was fighting and indeed winning the war on drugs. Some war. It was not even a fist fight.

Meanwhile, despite growing evidence, the public has been treated to years of limp Bush denials that he "wasn't in the loop" on the Iran-contra weapons and drug deals that have repulsed the American public. Closer to home, Bush's sons have been involved in the large-scale looting of America's financial institutions.

In hindsight, this book should have been written prior to the 1988 elections. It has been extremely distressing to witness the American people and the world subjected to a systematic program of travesties pushed forward by the Bush administration.

Many of our current sociological and economic problems might have been less serious had we understood the hidden agenda that Bush and his hangers-on have cruelly unleashed upon our country.

It should come as no surprise to readers, the Bush Administration has not made it easy for Americans to find out the truth. While researching this book, for example, the author discovered that the records and correspondence of Samuel Bush, George's grandfather who ran the arms-related section of the War Industries Board in 1918, had been burned "to save space" in the

National Archives. It's one more indication of how George Bush may be one of the most "covert" presidents in American history.

New York Times columnist Tom Wicker raised the question, "Do the American people really want to elect a former director of the CIA as their president?" back on April 18, 1988. "That's hardly been discussed so far," he wrote. "But it seems obvious that a CIA chief might well be privy to the kind of 'black secrets' that could later make him as a public figure subject to blackmail."

"Given the agency's worldwide reputation for covert information and political meddling, moreover, one of its former directors in the White House certainly would be the object of suspicion and mistrust in numerous parts of the globe. And well might be."

Insight from the months of painstaking preparation of this manuscript allow me to state unequivocally that George Bush is utterly beholden to establishment and special interests, especially oil. Since this is an unauthorized work, the writer has been forced to labor under severe constraints of time and expense. But the author hopes that by seeing the real face of George Bush in the following pages, Americans will realize the grand deception that has been played on them. Only by knowing the truth, and by seeing the real George Bush and his self-serving agenda, can Americans be freed from the deceptions they have so long been forced to endure.

CHAPTER 1

In the Name of the Father

"War is just a racket"

**Major General Smedley Butler,
former Commandant of the U.S. Marine Corps**

"And what does it amount to?" said Satan, with his evil chuckle. "Nothing at all. You gain nothing: you always come out where you went in. For a million years the race has gone on monotonously propagating itself and monotonously reperforming this dull nonsense to what end? No wisdom can guess! Who gets a profit out of it? Nobody but a parcel of usurping little monarchs and nobilities who despise you; would feel defiled if you touched them; would shut the door in your face if you proposed to call; whom you slave for, fight for, die for, and are not ashamed of it, but proud; whose existence is a perpetual insult to you and you are afraid to resent it; who are mendicants supported by your alms, yet assume toward you the airs of benefactor toward beggar; who address you in the language of master toward slave, and are answered in the language of slave toward master; who are worshipped by you with your mouth, while in your heart if you have one you despise yourselves for it. The first man was a hypocrite and a coward, qualities which have not failed yet in his line; it is the foundation upon which all civilizations have been built..."

Mark Twain in *The Mysterious Stranger*

1

*"Those who do not understand history are condemned
to repeat it."*

George Santayana, philosopher and writer

While Democratic candidate Michael Dukakis spent most of
the 1988 presidential campaign trying to dodge the liberal label,
George Bush and the Republican National Committee have
carefully rejected any discussion of the "N-word" through three
national campaigns. This is not at all surprising, in light of the
fact that Bush's closest friend and confidante is Texas mystery
man William Stamps Farish III, inheritor of the Auschwitz death
camp fortune.

When he was elected vice president in 1980, Bush desig-
nated Farish to manage all of his personal wealth in a "blind
trust." As one of the richest men in Texas, Farish keeps his own
business affairs secret. Bush knows that he can rely on Farish to
keep the secrets about his own family money, since Farish's
family fortune was made in the same Nazi enterprise with
George Bush's father.

Farish's grandfather, W.S. Farish, pleaded "no contest" in
1942 to charges of criminal conspiracy with the Nazis. As
president and chief executive of Standard Oil of New Jersey,
Farish was the controller of the global cartel between Standard
Oil and the German I.G. Farben concern.

The joint enterprise had opened the Auschwitz slave labor
camp on June 14, 1940, to produce artificial rubber and gasoline
from coal. Jews and political opponents supplied by Hitler as
slaves were worked to death or murdered.

Senator Harry S. Truman headed a Senate committee investigating the corporations' collaboration with the Nazis. Farish
was brought before the committee to answer questions concerning his company's alliance with the Hitler regime that had
begun with his presidency of Jersey Standard in 1933.

Before Farish testified, Truman told newsmen, "I think this

approaches treason." In fact, Standard Oil's dealings with Hitler continued right up to the end of World War II.

In September of 1988, revelations concerning the pro-Nazi, fascist and anti-Semitic backgrounds of members of the Bush presidential campaign led to the resignation or firing of seven high-ranking officials in the ethnic-outreach program.

The seven were part of the GOP's recruitment of the most extreme rightwing elements in the Eastern European ethnic communities of the United States. The party encouraged participation by its ethnic Heritage Groups Council, the fundraising clique to which the seven anti-Semites belonged since at least 1949. In fact an RNC internal memorandum shows that George Bush, while GOP national chairman in 1973, had full knowledge of and, in the words of the memo, provided "total support" for the party's ethnic Heritage Groups.

The charges against several of the fundraisers were not new: On November 21, 1971, the eve of the Watergate break-in, *The Washington Post* exposed Richard Nixon's Heritage Groups, two years before Bush became Chairman of the Republican National Committee.

Bush has repeatedly professed ignorance of the pro-Nazi backgrounds of these groups. Two of the individuals fired were also key figures in the Post revelations 21 years ago.

The top-level 1976 memorandum was written by Heritage Groups Director Col. Jay Niemczyk to the then RNC co-chairman Robert Carter praising Bush's leadership of the ethnic recruitment effort as having "added needed strength and impetus" to the Republicans' exploitation of transplanted Nazi collaborators and war criminals.

In addition to the Heritage Groups, however, the Republicans' pursuit of hardline anti-communist support included the enlistment of ancillary ethnic organizations to host campaign stops for the Republican Party, attend White House meetings and raise funds.

Two of the campaign staffers fired in 1988 were also key

figures in revelations by the *Post* 17 years before. Philip Guarino, a former Roman Catholic priest, was charged with being a member of the Italian fascist group known as P-2. Laszlo Pastor admitted having been a member of the Hungarian fascist party, the Arrow/Cross, and having been an Arrow/Cross envoy to Nazi Germany during World War II.

Yaroslav Stetsko (who died in 1985) was Bush's ally with perhaps the closest ties to Hitler's Germany. An extreme Ukrainian nationalist, he collaborated with the Nazis in World War II as the very short-term "prime minister" of the "independent" Ukrainian puppet government set up in Galicia, or the Western Lands of the Ukraine.

Captured Nazi documents revealed that more than 100,000 Jews were exterminated in the Galician capital of Lvov within two years of the establishment of Stesko's regime.

According to official U.S. and Allied policies on the treatment of unsuspected war criminals and collaborators, each of the four organizations of which he was an activist leader were proscribed, and their members barred from entering the United States and subject to arrest on sight as suspected war criminals. One such group, the Anti-Bolshevik Bloc of Nations (ABN), participated in a 1983 White House meeting with Reagan and Bush. A photograph he retained of the meeting was signed, "To the Honorable Yaroslav Stetsko, With Best Wishes, *George Bush.*"

The 1976 RNC memo demonstrates that a basic goal of the Heritage Groups Council through the last 40 years has been to maintain the anti-Soviet, anti-communist Cold War zeal of eastern European immigrants. The memo demonstrates that Bush not only knew about the workings of the Heritage Groups, he actually worked with their leaders.

It unmasked Bush's strategy in 1988 and again in 1992 of stonewalling revelations about the Nazi war criminal apologists. His employment in both campaigns of Fred Malek, a well-known Nazi collaborator, graphically underscores his lack of concern about the victims of Hitler's war machine.[1]

George Herbert Walker Bush springs from an old-line Connecticut family lineage with long-time connections to Wall Street international bankers, oil interests, *and* the fascist cartels behind the German Third Reich. The man who touts his status as part of the "old establishment" who "chose to seek his fortune as an independent oilman," was never "independent," nor is his family part of the Old Guard of the Eastern seaboard. The Bush family gained its influence, through associations developed by their willingness to do *anything* to advance their station with the more powerful families they served.

George's father, Prescott Sheldon Bush, was born in Columbus, Ohio, on May 15, 1885, son of the manufacturer Samuel Prescott and Flora (Sheldon) Bush. Young Prescott attended St. George's Episcopal prep school in Newport, Rhode Island and graduated from Yale University. Entering Yale in 1913, Prescott Bush was initiated into the secret powerful fraternity Skull & Bones in 1916.

Skull & Bones was a screening device by Wall Street financiers to acquire ambitious, trustworthy young men of proper lineage to perpetuate their version of British-like aristocracy. The cream of the crop, so to speak, of young WASP intelligentsia were brought into this Secret Society.

The munitions trade also served to elevate Prescott Bush and his father, Samuel P. Bush, into the lower ranks of the Eastern Establishment, through their association with the Remington Arms Company. In accordance with directives from the National City Bank in 1914 aimed at reorganizing the domestic arms industry, Percy Rockefeller took direct control of the Remington Arms Company, appointing as his chief executive Samuel F. Pryor.

Samuel Bush was appointed chief of the Ordnance, Small

---

1   Charles R. Allen, Jr., "The Real Nazis Behind Every Bush," *Village Voice*, November 1, 1988.

Arms and Ammunition Section of the War Industries Board in the spring of 1918, several months after the official U.S. entry into the war in Europe.[2] Wall Street speculator Bernard Baruch, who had close personal and business ties to E.H. Harriman, was in overall charge of the War Industries Board. Baruch's brokerage firm had handled a number of the older Harriman's investments.[3] On the other hand, Samuel Bush's entire career prior to this time had been in the railroad business, supplying equipment to railroad systems owned by Wall Street moguls. From his new position, Samuel Bush was responsible for directing government assistance to and maintaining relations with a large number of weapons companies, including Remington.

During World War I, Prescott Bush served as a captain in the 322nd Field Regiment of the U.S. Army Field Artillery. A story in his hometown newspaper describing in detail his being awarded three of the highest military honors for valor was later exposed as a prank by his own mother, Flora Sheldon Bush, in a letter to the editor. Following his discharge in 1919, Bush returned to his hometown, but the humiliation was so intense that he could not remain.[4]

He took an offer from a fellow Bonesman in the railroad equipment business and relocated his career with Simmons Hardware in St. Louis, Missouri. He worked with Stedman Products from 1922-1924 and from 1924-26 with United States Rubber Company.

During this period, Averill Harriman, still smarting over

---

2   Gen. Hugh S. Johnson to Major J.H.K. Davis, June 6, 1918, file no. 334.8/168 or 334.8/451 in the U.S. National Archives, Suitland, Maryland.

3   Bernard Baruch, *My Own Story* (New York: Henry Holt and Co., 1957), pp. 138-139.

4   *The Ohio State Journal*, August 9 and September 6, 1918. The "war hero" story was never permitted to be brought up in his presence thereafter. Decades later, when he was an important and wealthy U.S. senator, his fellow congressmen whispered about and puzzled over the story.

Theodore Roosevelt's excoriation of his father for "cynicism and deep-seated corruption," and his denunciation as an "undesirable citizen," created a financial and informational network to take his place in the pantheon of international power brokers.[5] Harriman's choice to establish this network was a Missouri stockbroker and wheeler-dealer named George Herbert "Bert" Walker, after whom our president is named.

By 1919 Walker had achieved preeminence as the Midwest's premier deal-fixer, always operating quietly behind the scenes in local and global affairs. Through his contacts with the Guaranty Trust Company in New York and to the British banking house of J.P. Morgan and Co., Walker achieved tremendous powers of patronage through awarding of investment capital to the railroads, utilities and other industries of which he and his associates in St. Louis were executives or board members.

The son of a dry goods wholesaler who had prospered through import trade with England, Walker inherited summer homes in Santa Barbara, Calif. and at "Walker's Point" in Kennebunkport, Maine.

The postwar global arrangements negotiated at the 1919 Versailles peace conference opened up staggering possibilities for the American and British imperialists. Harriman recognized Walker's cunning and influence among the British-anointed captains of U.S. finance and politics, and prevailed upon him to move to New York to implement his scheme. That November, the W.A. Harriman & Co. private bank was established by Walker, who became president and chief executive. Averill Harriman became chairman and controlling co-owner with his brother Roland, close friend by this time of Prescott Bush. Percy

---

5   Theodore Roosevelt to James S. Sherman, October 6, 1906, made public by Roosevelt at a press conference April 2, 1907. Quoted in Henry F. Pringle, *Theodore Roosevel*, (New York: Harcourt, Brace and Co., 1931), p. 452. Roosevelt later confided to Robert S. Lovett, Harriman's attorney, that his views on Harriman were based on what J.P. Morgan had told him.

Rockefeller was made a director in return for his substantial financial contribution.

During this same time period, Prescott Bush met Walker's daughter Dorothy. They were married in August, 1921.[6] Half of the 11 "ushers and groomsmen" in attendance at the wedding were Bush's fellow Skull and Bonesmen from 1917.

At that time Bush was a minor executive at the Simmons Co. railroad equipment suppliers, while his father-in-law was assembling one of the most gigantic business combines in the world. The couple returned to Bush's home in Columbus, Ohio, where he worked in his father's rubber products company, but the taint of his wartime activities haunted him. A short time later he moved to Milton, Mass., where his son, the future U.S. President George Herbert Walker Bush, was born on June 12, 1924.

Through the intercession of his Yalie friend, "Bunny" Harriman, on May 1, 1926, Prescott Bush was invited to join W.A. Harriman & Co. as its vice president, serving under the bank's president, his father-in-law, George Herbert Walker.

Prescott Bush would demonstrate strong loyalty to the firm, serving the Harriman interests the rest of his life.

Thus the "conservative" Prescott Bush was a fraternity and business partner of the "liberal" Harriman family; their common bond was internationalism. Using all the international connections at his disposal, young George's grandfather quietly created a banking structure which would wield as much influence as some nations.

Prescott Bush served later as a director of Columbia Broadcasting System, Inc., the Prudential Company of America, Dresser Industries, Inc., Hydrocarbon Research Inc., Union Banking Corp., Vanadium Corp. of America and the U.S. Guaranty Trust

---

6   Prescott Bush, Interview by the Oral History Research Project conducted by Columbia University in 1966, Eisenhower Administration Part II; pp. 5-6. The interview was supposed to be kept secret and was never published, but Columbia later sold microfilms of the transcript to certain libraries, including Arizona State University.

among other companies until 1952, when he successfully ran for the U.S. Senate from Connecticut. He was re-elected in 1962.

The significance of these corporations is their role in the buildup of both the Soviet Union *and* Nazi Germany. Dresser Industries is a prominent manufacturer of oil drilling equipment vitally needed to expand Soviet oil fields and Dresser has been in the forefront to make the USSR the Number One world oil producer. Oil is its greatest single source of foreign exchange. Guaranty Trust was also a link with the Soviet Union, as was W.A. Harriman and Company with its Georgian Manganese Concession in the 1920s.

Most conspicuously absent from all the official Bush biographies, however, is the role of Prescott Bush and his fellow Skull & Bones members in the creation of the Nazi war machine itself through Union Banking Corporation and its Nazi affiliates.

In 1920, Averill Harriman announced that he would revive Germany's Hamburg-Amerika Line, confiscated by the United States at the end of the First World War. As the result of behind-the-scenes arrangements with U.S. Authorities, the Harriman group had gained control of the ships.

The world's largest private shipping line was created, through purchase of the confiscated vessels, and the extension to the Harriman bank of "the right to participate" in 50 percent of all business originated in Hamburg. Harriman maintained "complete control of all activities of the Hamburg line in the United States" for 20 years.[7] The Harriman-Walker firm, as co-owner of Hamburg-Amerika, maintained this control with the support of the British and U.S. armies of occupation.

The requisite financial backing came from a "marriage" engineered by Walker of credit from the J.P. Morgan companies and inherited wealth from the Harriman family, through the merging of W. A. Harriman & Co. with the Morton & Co.

---

7   Averell Harriman, public statement in the *New York Times,* October 6, 1920, p.1.

private bank, which was interlocked with the Guaranty Trust Co. controlled by Morgan.

From this base in Berlin, Harriman and Walker worked with the new dictatorship of the Soviet Union. The Russian oil industry, which had been devastated by the Bolshevik Revolution, received a major infusion of capital from the Wall Street and British Empire speculators headed by Walker and Harriman.[8] They also contracted with the Soviets to mine manganese, an essential component in steel manufacturing; first, directly through Leon Trotsky, then through Feliks Dzerzhinsky, founder of the dictatorship's secret intelligence service (KGB),

Prescott Bush maintained a fierce loyalty to the Harriman interests he served from 1926 onward, gradually positioning himself to run the day-to-day operations of W.A. Harriman & Co. Following the company's merger in 1931 with Brown Brothers, the British-American banking house, Prescott Bush became managing partner of the resulting company, Brown Brothers Harriman, which would become the largest and most politically influential private banking house in the United States.

When Bush lost the small fortune he had accumulated in the stock market crash of 1929, the Harrimans bankrolled Prescott Bush to the full extent of his lost fortune and put him in charge of managing their gigantic personal investment funds.[9] Prescott Bush was able to enlarge this fortune, which was inherited by his son, George, during these years between the two world wars through his involvement in the international project which the U.S. government itself would finally halt, the creation of Adolf Hitler's Wehrmacht.

Hitler received his backing from foreign and domestic sources including the Fritz Thyssen interests. When interrogated in 1945 under Project Dustbin, Thyssen recalled that in 1923 he

---

8   Dr. Antony Sutton, *Wall Street and the Bolshevik Revolution* (Veritas: Western Australia, 1981).

9   Prescott Bush, Columbia University, op. cit., pp. 16-22.

was approached by General Ludendorf, shortly after which he was introduced to Hitler and became a conduit for funds from Ludendorf for the building up of the fledgling National Socialist Party. Through Rudolf Hess, Thyssen arranged for a 250,000-mark credit for the Nazis via the Bank Voor Handel en Scheepvaart N.V. in Rotterdam, Holland. This bank was a subsidiary of Thyssen's bank (formerly von der Heyd's bank) in Germany and affiliated with the Harriman banking interests in New York. The Dutch bank controlled the Union Banking Corporation in New York and was indeed a joint Thyssen-Harriman operation with several of Prescott Bush's Skull & Bones initiates as directors.

In the 1930s Union Banking Corporation had the following directors:

E. Roland Harriman – Vice President of W.A. Harriman & Company and fellow Club member Skull & Bones with Prescott Bush

H.J. Kouwenhoven – Nazi banker and Managing Director of the Bank Voor Handel

J.G. Groeningen – Nazi member of the steel cartel that also financed Hitler

C. Lievense – President, Union Banking Corporation, New York

E.S. James – Partner of W.A. Harriman and fellow initiate in the Prescott Bush 1917 cell of Skull & Bones

Prescott Bush – Director of Union Banking Corp.

An example of Brown Brothers, Harriman's assistance to Nazi Germany was their underwriting of Standard Oil agreements in cooperation with General Motors to supply ethyl lead to the Nazis. Ethyl fluid is an anti-knock compound that improves engine efficiency.

The I.G. Farben files captured at the end of the war confirm the importance of this particular technical transfer for the German Wehrmacht:

Since the beginning of the war we have been in a position to produce lead tetraethyl solely because, a short time before the outbreak of the war, the Americans had established plants for us ready for production and supplied us with all available experience. In this manner we did not need to perform the difficult work of development because we could start production right away on the basis of all the experience that the Americans had for years.[10]

In 1938, just before the outbreak of war in Europe, the German Luftwaffe urgently needed 500 tons of tetraethyl lead (Ethyl) for military purposes. This 500 tons was loaned by the Ethyl Export Corporation of New York to Ethyl G.m.b.H. of Germany, in a transaction arranged by the Reich Air Ministry with I.G. Farben director Mueller-Cunradi. The collateral security was arranged in a letter dated September 21, 1938 through *Brown Brothers, Harriman & Co. of New York.*

Prescott Bush was a lifelong partner in Brown Brothers, Harriman. W. Averell Harriman had a longtime association with the Soviet Union. As early as 1922 Harriman, with Guaranty Trust, was financing Soviet deals. In winding up his Manganese Concession in 1929, Harriman received a windfall profit from the Soviets. State Department officials were uncertain how to classify this gift, but never investigated it.

The conclusion is that the Harrimans and Prescott Bush were intimately associated with financing the Nazis *and* the Soviets, both representing the farthest extreme from American principles.

---

10 Dr. Antony Sutton, *Wall Street and the Rise of Hitler* (Seal Beach, Calif.:'76 Press, 1976), p. 74. The entire story is examined in far greater detail in this volume and Dr. Sutton's other watershed work, *Wall Street and the Bolshevik Revolution.*

CHAPTER 2

And of the Son

From this elite Eastern Establishment of politicians, businessmen and financiers exerting their influence in America's foreign and domestic policies, sprang George Bush.

By every standard of measure, he represents, reflects and nurtures the elitism of his forefathers and their cronies. Yet his 30-year career has been a dichotomy.

- Scion of a wealthy WASP Establishment family with homes in Connecticut and Maine.
- Self-made, rugged individualist, oilman, khaki shirt, sleeves rolled up.
- Right wing conservative politician holding firmly to the rigid principles of the Republican party.
- Modern, insightful centrist Republican, willing to open the party doors to all windows of thought.

Take your pick of the aforementioned, and you will not be wrong. George Bush, it seems, desperately seeks to be all things to all people.

As one of Florida's top Republican officials said: "George has no center. He stands for nothing. He is a political opportunist in the truest sense of the word."

What makes this strange political animal tick?

That may be impossible to answer. Certainly his background was of elegance and comfort, thanks to the unscrupulous business tactics of his father.

When the rest of the country was plunged into the Great Depression following the stock market crash of 1929, George Bush and his family flourished thanks to the largesse of Averell

Harriman and the massive profits from Grandfather Walker's oil deals with the Soviets and the financial arrangements between Brown Brothers Harriman and the Thyssen-Nazi cartels. The Bushes were cushioned from the suffering endured by the majority of Americans. The Hamburg-Amerika steamship line, whose work force was controlled by the Nazi Labor Front, poured money into the Walker and Bush coffers.

The Bushes lived in a large, dark-shingled house with broad verandas on Grove Lane in the Deer Park section of Greenwich, Conn.[1] They were attended by four servants, three maids and a chauffeur. The family spent its summers at the second home built by Grandfather Walker at Kennebunkport, Maine. Along with the colony's other well-to-do inhabitants, the Bush kids learned tennis and sailing at Kennebunkport River Club.

George was named after his grandfather, George Herbert Walker, who was called "Pop" by George's mother. She gave George what became his lifelong nickname when she began calling him "little Pop," or "Poppy."

Poppy's mother and father raised him and his siblings, older brother Prescott, Jr., younger sister Nancy, and brothers Jonathan and William, to be mindful of their family's distinguished lineage and its growing importance in the world.[2]

As the world economic crisis deepened, and other Americans were experiencing unprecedented hardship and fear, the Bush children were taught that those who suffered had no one to blame but themselves. Writer, Joe Hyams, glowingly recounted Bush's roots in 1991 based on material supplied by the White

---

1   Nicholas King, *George Bush: A Biography* (New York: Dodd, Mead & Co., 1980), pp. 13-14.

2   Joe Hyams, *Flight of the Avenger* (New York: Harcourt, Brace Jovanovich, 1991), p. 14. "Prescott Sheldon Bush, George's father, was a third-generation American who could trace his family's roots back to England's King Henry III, making George a thirteenth cousin, twice removed, of Queen Elizabeth II."

House: "Alec, the family chauffeur, drove the two boys to school every morning after dropping Prescott, Sr., at the railroad station for the morning commute to Manhattan. The Depression was nowhere in evidence as the boys glided in the family's black Oldsmobile past the stone fences, stables, and swimming pools of one of the wealthiest communities in America."

Prescott Bush, who was heaping the family fortunes through sophisticated bond deals with John Foster Dulles for the Nazis, was, according to Hyams, "a thrifty man who daily impressed on his children the value of a dollar and encouraged frugality and saving. He had no sympathy for the nouveau riches who flaunted their wealth, they were without class, he said. As a sage and strictly honest businessman, he had often turned failing companies around, making them profitable again, and he had scorn for people who went bankrupt because they mismanaged their money."

George Bush left his day school in Greenwich at age 12 to join his older brother at Phillips Academy in Andover, Massachusetts, 20 miles north of Boston. "Andover" was one of the most exclusive of the New England preparatory or "prep" schools, whose students were almost without exception wealthy, Episcopalian white boys. As Bush's own staff conceded in a 1980 campaign biography, "At the close of the 1930s...these schools...brought the famous 'old-boy networks' to the peak of their power."[3]

Bush's own military career in World War II was relatively uneventful but offers unlimited opportunities for image promoters. On his 18th birthday Bush enlisted in the Naval reserve. After flight training at Corpus Christi, Texas, the 20-year-old Navy pilot was assigned to the Third and Fifth Fleets in the Pacific.

While serving on the light aircraft carrier USS *San Jacinto*, the TMB-3E Avenger torpedo bomber flown by Bush, was shot down by anti-aircraft fire.

---

3   King, pp. 13-14.

Bush bailed out, leaving the other crew members to fend for themselves, even though the Avenger was built to sustain ocean-crash landings. He was picked up four hours later by the U.S. submarine *Finback*. He describes in his autobiography, "Later I learned that neither Jack Delaney nor Ted White had survived. One went down with the plane; the other was seen jumping, but his parachute failed to open.[4]

The decorated Bush was discharged in 1945 with the rank of Lieutenant (j.g.). This portrayal has been pushed scores of times into the media under various excuses to pump up the 'Bush the War hero' image. On September 3, 1984, for example, this relatively minor episode in the Pacific was converted into an anniversary at Norfolk Naval Base. Bush was photographed waving from a vintage Avenger and took the opportunity to make an "I was there" speech.

In the speech, Bush reminded his naval audience: "I think all of us who have seen combat know how important that techno-logical edge is. When you have to go up there alongside the enemy and alone against the enemy you don't want someone to be cutting corners on the equipment."

Ann Lewis, political director of the Democratic National Committee, criticized the Norfolk Naval Base episode, "I think events like this for the purpose of a national campaign trivialize the very values that they claim to defend. That a politician would order a special Navy anniversary organized to trumpet his own brief military endeavors is trivial and hypocritical indeed."[5]

After leaving the Navy in 1946, Bush contracted what has been called a "corporate merger" type of marriage, popular in the 1940s and 1950s when powerful groups intermarried for power more than any other reason. George Bush married Bar-

---

4   George Bush with Victor Gold, *Looking Forward* (Doubleday: New York, 1987), pp.36-39.

5   Sutton, *The Two Faces of George Bush* (New York: Wiswell Ruffin House, Inc., 1988), p.6.

bara Pierce, Smith College educated, daughter of the publisher Marvin Pierce of *McCalls* Magazine.

It was Barbara Pierce's brother Scott Pierce, President of E.F. Hutton, who was in the center of the E.F. Hutton check-kiting scandals that cost American investors millions of dollars over an extended period in the 1980's. In May 1985, Scott Pierce pled guilty to mail fraud charges.

According to syndicated columnist Jack Anderson, Scott Pierce, through other E.F. Hutton associates, asked Vice President Bush to intervene. Given the extraordinarily light nature of the sentences, there were *2,000 counts of mail fraud* and *no one* went to prison, it seems certain that someone in power successfully intervened. However, crucial documentation of the Vice President lunching with his brother-in-law and discussing the case is not available.

Like his father before him, George Bush's biography pays scant attention to his 1948 membership in Skull & Bones, a society so secret that virtually nothing is known about it or its membership.

One researcher has spent several years in an unsuccessful attempt to have Bush admit this membership and present an open book to the electorate about his oath of allegiance to this secret society.

Club 1948 contains George Herbert Walker Bush, who, with 14 fellow brothers, chose the Club of 1949. The Club of 1949 includes Reverend William Sloane Coffin Jr., the anti-war cleric with a decidedly off-beat revolutionary fervor based at the old-time Riverside Church, New York. Sometimes it appears that everything stemming from Marxist revolution in the U.S. also stems from Riverside Church. In the same cell as revolutionary Coffin is C.E. Lord (generations of Lord families have always had representatives in Skull & Bones). This Lord was Comptroller of the Currency. P.W. Lufkin of the firm Donaldson, Lufkin and Jenrette V. Van Dine was a long-term CIA operative, as was William Sloane Coffin. All however, are sworn by common oath not to divulge their activities.

After leaving the U.S. Navy, Bush started his business career in Texas oil as a salesman for Neil Mallon of Dresser Industries of Dallas, Texas, the oil supply company with links to the Soviet Union that his father had previously managed. Bush began employment in Odessa, Texas with one of Dresser's subsidiaries, Ideco (short for International Derrick and Equipment Company). In his autobiography, Bush described his advent in the Texas oilfields this way: "Heading into Texas in my Studebaker, all I knew about the state's landscape was what I'd seen from the cockpit of a Vultee Vibrator during my training days in the Navy."[6]

Fitzhugh Green, in his *George Bush: An Intimate Portrait*, published after Bush became president, described the Studebaker trip: "He [Bush] gassed up his 1948 Studebaker, arranged for his wife and son to follow, and headed for Odessa, Texas."

A 1983 Texas magazine article written by Harry Hurt III carried this description, "When George Herbert Walker Bush drove his battered red Studebaker into Odessa in the summer of 1948, the town's population, though constantly increasing with newly-arrived oil hands, was still under 30,000." Several other versions of the Studebaker story have been reprinted in other biographies of Bush and his wife, Barbara.

The only problem with this story is that Bush did not arrive in Odessa, Texas in a red Studebaker. Texas oilman and Bush campaign contributor Oscar Wyatt of Houston attempted to correct the story in a letter to the *Texas Monthly*, in which he specified that "when people speak of Mr. Bush's humble beginnings in the oil industry, it should be noted that he rode down to Texas on Dresser's private aircraft. He was accompanied by his father who at the time was one of the directors of Dresser Industries.... I hate it when people make statements about Mr. Bush's humble beginnings in the oil industry. It just didn't

---

6   George Bush with Victor Gold, p. 47.

happen that way."

After less than a year in Odessa, Dresser Industries trans-ferred Bush to California where he worked as a salesman selling Ideco drilling bits. Bush then teamed with John Overby, an independent operator, in his own oil and gas lease business as President of Bush-Overby Development Company based in Midland, Texas, incorporated in Delaware in 1953 and merged with Walker-Bush Corporation in 1955. One of his key inves-tors was Eugene Meyer, owner of the *Washington Post*, who held a number of accounts with Brown Brothers, Harriman.

The Bush family's mingling of business, politics and intelli-gence re-started in 1953 when Bush co-founded his own oil company, Zapata Petroleum Corp. of Houston, Texas in partner-ship with Hugh and Bill Liedtke. Bush described the merger thusly:

"The following year it would spin off into Zapata Off-Shore, and in time, under Hugh Liedtke's imaginative management, merge into Pennzoil. Zapata: There was a winning chemistry about the company. We could sense it."[7]

Zapata Off-Shore Company, founded with Bush as Presi-dent and Liedtke as treasurer, became a highly successful opera-tor in offshore drilling for oil. Typically, Zapata had the advan-tages of Bush investment-banking connections and family wealth. Starting in 1953 from an initial investment of $500,000 each from Bush-Overby and the Liedtke brothers, according to Bush, Zapata's 1985 Annual report listed revenues of well over one-quarter billion dollars from a fleet of offshore drilling rigs.

This relatively unknown company today employs 7,300 people, not bad for a 30-year-old company built from an idea.

---

7   See "The Roar of the Crowd," *Texas Monthly*, November, 1991. See also Jan Garble, "Meaner Than a Junkyard Dog," *Texas Monthly*, April 1991, p. 68 ff. Wyatt observes, "I knew from the beginning George Bush came to Texas only because he was politically ambitious. He flew out here on an airplane owned by Dresser Industries. His daddy was a member of the board of Dresser."

However, Zapata owes its success to an ability to negotiate contracts with large international oil companies in competition with 140 other offshore drilling companies. Zapata has taken advantage of government financing programs and especially U.S. government-guaranteed ship-financing securities at 8 3/4 percent, subsidized by the U.S. taxpayer.

Bush served as president of Zapata Oil from 1954 to 1964 and then as Chairman of the Board of Zapata Off-Shore from 1964 to 1966. In brief, Bush's money came from Texas oil.

In this he was always associated with Hugh Liedtke, who came to prominence when Bush was Republican national chairman in 1973 and it was revealed that the Texas campaign fund of Bush's former partner, Liedtke, had been used to partly finance the Watergate break-in.

In 1977, Bush and Liedtke went to China, Bush in an official capacity. Knowing this, the Chinese made their confidential oil surveys available to Liedtke's oil company, the only one to receive these surveys. This gesture was presumably because of Bush's position.

More recently Pennzoil, a Liedtke company, received the largest damages award in American history. Texaco was charged with interfering with a merger deal made by Pennzoil and Getty.

For this, the judge awarded a phenomenal $12 billion in damages, a sum that if paid could have broken Texaco. No one has investigated possible Bush influence on the subsequent appeal which was settled at $4 billion.

While Bush was vice president, his son, George Jr. became President of Zapata Off-Shore. This helps explain why the Vice President flew to the Middle East in early 1986 to persuade the Arab countries to raise the price of oil which had, to the delight of the average citizen, fallen below a dollar a gallon.

Bush used the argument to the Arabs that U.S. security depended on a rise in the price of crude oil, then $12 a barrel on the spot market. With operating costs at $2 a barrel, the Arabs were making $8 to $10 a barrel but this was not enough for the Vice

President and his Texas oil friends. This Middle East Bush visit triggered consternation in the White House. Here was the Vice President of an administration devoted to free markets encouraging use of underhanded practices to raise the price of crude.

The Reagan administration hastened to put some distance between itself and a Vice President who apparently only got tough when crude oil prices started to fall to the advantage of the American consumer.

Said another official: "Look, the policy is and remains free market, that's the core of the policy…the reason there's no oil import fee is because the decisive vote against it was cast by Ronald Reagan." There were even concerns that in helping raise oil-prices, Bush was "digging himself a political hole" for 1988.

This prompted Bush to claim: "I'm in a listening mode when it comes to the intentions of these major producing countries. And again the interest in the United States is bound to be cheap energy if we possibly can. But from our interest there is some point where the national security interests of the United States say, 'Hey, we must have a strong viable domestic industry.'"[8]

This is surely political double-talk. When we needed the help of the Saudi Arabians in 1987 during the Iraqi raid on the *U.S.S. Stark*, they refused to aid us. Furthermore it was Dresser Industries, founded with friends of the Bush family, that has provided the majority of assistance in expanding Soviet crude oil production to compete with U.S. and Arab crude. The only time one finds tough behavior on the part of George Bush is when oil interests and family business interests are at stake.

Crude oil prices promptly rose $2 a barrel after Bush's visit to the Middle East. This action on behalf of big oil accounts for the increased oil-company contributions to the Bush Political Action Committee (PAC), Fund for America's Future. Probably one third of the contributions come from Midland, Dallas and Houston, Texas.

---

8   Sutton, *The Two Faces of George Bush*, p. 29.

Also curious is Bush's relationship with another former oilman, Jorge Diaz Serrano. In 1960, Bush went into a joint venture with Diaz Serrano in a Mexican drilling company called Permargo. Bush's 50 percent interest was hidden because his ownership violated Mexican law.

Permargo had lucrative contracts with Pemex, the giant state oil monopoly of Mexico.

Diaz Serrano went on to head Pemex from 1975 to 1980. After reports of Pemex being looted of billions during his reign, Diaz Serrano, who was reported to have lent Pemex as a cover for CIA covert operations in Mexico, was convicted in 1983 of defrauding the government. Bush's former partner spent five years in prison.

When *Barron's* financial magazine looked into what it called Bush's "shadowy Mexican operation," investigative reporter Jonathan Kwitny found that the Zapata records of Bush's relationship with Diaz Serrano, 1960-66, had been "inadvertently destroyed" by the SEC after Bush became vice president in 1981.

This is another example of Bush's success traced to family connections combined with government financing and intervention, rather than American free enterprise. It is, however, in the political field that the real, elitist, favored-son George Bush shines.

George Bush has had a remarkable political career. Bush apparently tackles a political objective, falls flat on his face, and then is eased by his elitist friends into a more coveted position by political appointment, such as his directorship of the CIA.

Bush's autobiography skips the early 1960s, except when he makes his official entry into public life as chair of the Harris County, Texas, Republican Party in 1963 and as a Texas delegate to the 1964 Republican National Convention.

He ran unsuccessfully for the Senate in 1964 against the "liberal" Democratic incumbent Ralph Yarborough. In his first major political outing, Bush wore the mantle of a Goldwater Republican, campaigning against the Nuclear Test Ban Treaty,

Medicare, allowing Red China into the United Nations, and the Civil Rights Act. Beating off conservative primary candidates, Bush grabbed the Republican nomination, only to lose to Yarborough by 300,000 votes. Nevertheless, Bush attracted 43 percent of the vote, a good showing in a state where Democrats far outnumbered Republicans.

Bush "quit" the oil business in 1966 and with backing from family, friends and the establishment business community, was elected to Congress from a safe affluent Houston district. His voting record in Congress was mixed, certainly not straight Goldwaterite.

From that point Bush adopted what has become known as the Eastern Establishment position, a weak unprincipled mishmash of policies that has brought no-win war and economic chaos to the United States.

As a freshman Congressman with elitist backing, Bush immediately was given a coveted seat on the House Ways and Means Committee. It was reported on Sept. 28, 1986 in *Washington Post Magazine* that Bush got this seat through pressure from chairman Democrat Wilbur Mills and then Leader of the House Republican Jerry Ford. According to a 1980 *Rolling Stone* article, Mills took a liking to Bush, nicknaming him "Rubbers" for his support of family planning.

A public appearance of conservatism can be traced throughout the Bush political career but that is inconsistent with his voting records and political actions. By 1970 Bush had a record that a conservative Democratic businessman, Lloyd Bentsen, could misrepresent as "liberal." The two faced off in a Senate contest in Texas after Bentsen defeated the liberal Yarborough in a vicious primary.

Bush was encouraged to enter the race by President Nixon, who had targeted Southern liberals, including Yarborough, for defeat.

Under a cloak of Goldwater conservatism, Bush actually held left-liberal political opinions supporting gun control, for example, while opposing repeal of the Federal Income Tax, and further military involvement in Vietnam.

Expecting to face Yarborough in the general election, Bush was unprepared for Bentsen, who castigated him for his support of gun control and a guaranteed annual income for the poor. Bush, the eager beaver, had waited only two terms in the House before running again for the Senate in 1970 only to lose and throw away the opportunities brought by family and business contacts.

Once again, privilege came to George's assistance. To throw away a safe Congressional seat on a gamble for the Senate would seem to demonstrate a severe lack of judgment, yet it was rewarded by the Establishment with a coveted appointment. In February 1971 Bush became Ambassador to the United Nations. There he took up an old cause: keeping China out of that body. While Bush argued for China's exclusion, Henry Kissinger conducted secret negotiations with Beijing to revive U.S.-Sino relations.

In January 1973 Bush's political career was boosted once again. Nixon appointed him Chairman of the Republican National Committee, where he campaigned for a quick end to the Senate Watergate hearings and loyally defended his patron.

Instead of choosing a seasoned, strategist, Nixon picked a two-time Senate loser who needed influence to make his way in Congress and a loser who was deeply suspect by constitutionalists within the Republican party.

After eighteen months at the National Committee, Bush again ached for change and without leaving any memorial at the RNC, was appointed envoy to the People's Republic of China, to replace an ailing David Bruce.

This came about because of the Nixon-Kissinger change of face, i.e. to treat Communist China as an ally rather than a threat to the United States. However, as more than one commentator has observed, principle is not a George Bush hallmark. His approach has been called "guiltless pragmatism," in other words, a shifting of position irrespective of principle.

A year later Ford called him home to head the Central Intelligence Agency. Bush's appointment as the Agency's director in 1975 was widely criticized because, as Bush writes, "Bill Colby, a professional in the intelligence field, was being replaced by a nonprofessional outsider and a politician to boot."

Senator Frank Church commented: "It appears as though the White House may be using this important post merely as a grooming room before he is brought on stage next year as a vice-presidential running mate." Speaking against the appointment, Church said he knew of "no particular reason why [Bush] is qualified" for the job.

Since it is very likely that Church did not know of Bush's earlier connections to the CIA, his reaction was understandable. But Bush needed a position. So once again "guiltless pragmatism" won over principles.

CHAPTER 3

Operation Zapata
"The Bay of Pigs Thing"

Actually, however, Congress was being manipulated. This is how the war machine operates. Behind the seeming concern for national security are the busy men with the bulging briefcases hurrying from the Pentagon over to Capitol Hill, the tight-mouthed men hurrying from CIA headquarters over to the Pentagon; it is eventually a game. It is an operation designed to produce for the warfare sector and its military hardware supporters billions of dollars annually and unlimited power in the affairs of the nation.

Since the end of World War II, the United States has spent a thousand billion dollars — one trillion dollars — furnished by the American people, who have been colonized by these men and their hunger for power. Could the CIA kill a President to keep such an operation going? Kings have been beheaded for infinitely less.

Jim Garrison, *A Heritage of Stone* **(1970)**

"I mean, draw your own conclusions. There's a table of organization at the Company. The only people who had all the pieces in place that could have done it were a tight 'old-boy' network of guys that wanted to see him go, that thought he was committing suicide."

Former CIA agent Gordon Novel

JFK, Academy-Award winning film director Oliver Stone's three-hour, high-voltage inquisition into the assassination of John F. Kennedy, is the most controversial film in recent history. While the cameras were still rolling, on the basis of a first-draft script, *The Washington Post* skewered the film in an article titled "Dallas in Wonderland." Since then, almost every major newspaper, magazine and television commentator has voiced criticism of Stone's vision of a vast conspiracy behind the assassination.

Stone has retorted that "Every paper and magazine in America has devoted more space in the last three months to attacking my attack on the Warren Commission than they devoted in the previous 28 years to examining the Warren Commission.... My question is, 'Why are they so scared of this movie?' What are they defending?"[1]

Asked about the controversy, President Bush reiterated his faith in the Warren Commission, comparing conspiracy theories to rumors that Elvis is alive. Stone promptly fired off a statement to *Daily Variety* virtually accusing Bush of being part of the cover-up. In his 30 years in the "executive branch establishment," Stone writes, Bush "has had ample opportunity to stonewall the American people."[2]

"Dean, does Bush know about the [smoking gun] transcript yet?"
"Yes."
"Well, what did he do?"
"He broke out into assholes and shit himself to death."

Conversation between White House Congressional liaison William Timmons and Dean Burch, White House counselor as recorded in Woodward and Bernstein's *The Final Days*

---

1   Allen Barrio and Ty Burr, "JFK," *Entertainment Weekly*, January 17, 1992, p. 14.

2   Ibid, p. 16.

Bush's character, or lack thereof, was never more graphically demonstrated than the moment referred to above on August 5, 1974, during a meeting with other White House officials to assess the impact of the "smoking gun" tape. The recording contained the conversation between Nixon and chief of staff, H.R. Haldeman, held shortly after the original break-in at the Watergate, which could now no longer be contained. It was already understood among the men gathered to listen that Nixon's resignation was inevitable.

Bush's great concern, however, was not for his boss, Richard Nixon. His overpowering fear was that the smoking gun tape called attention to a money laundering mechanism which he, along with Bill Liedtke and Robert Mosbacher, Bush's partner, had helped to set up at Nixon's request in Mexico.

During that exchange, on June 23, 1972, Nixon told Haldeman to order Richard Helms at the CIA to stop the FBI's investigation into the transfer of funds from Texas and Minnesota through Mexico City into the coffers of the Committee to Re-Elect the President (CREEP), and from there into the hands of the "Plumbers" arrested in the Watergate building.

The statements on the tape were widely interpreted to constitute a *prima facie* case of obstruction of justice against Nixon. Bush's concern centered around Nixon's references to "the Texans," and "some Texas people," of whom Bush, Liedtke and Mosbacher were most prominent. The potential threat to Bush's political ambitions was staggering.

Bush, along with Nixon, was extremely concerned that the FBI's investigation would expose their connection to "the Bay of Pigs thing."

In the same discussion Nixon links "the Cubans," "the Texans," "Helms," "Hunt," "Bernard Barker, "Robert Mosbacher" and "the Bay of Pigs." Over and over on the Watergate tapes, these names come up in the discussions of the photos from

Dallas that Nixon was supposedly trying to obtain in the Watergate burglary. [3]

On the transcript Nixon describes George Bush's partner, Robert Mosbacher, as one of the Texas fundraisers for Nixon. Nixon refers to the "Cubans" and the "Texans." The "Texans" were Bush, Mosbacher, and Liedtke.

In fact, most of the CIA leadership in the planned invasion of Cuba seems to have been from Texas. An entire Texan branch of the CIA is based in the oil business.

If we trace Bush's background in the Texas oil business we discover his two partners in the oil-barge leasing business: Mosbacher and Texan James Baker. Mosbacher is now Secretary of Commerce and Baker is Secretary of State. According to a longtime operative in Agency operations in the Caribbean and South America, Bush's company, Zapata Oil, was one of the key suppliers of oil to Cuba under Batista.

After his landslide victory in 1972, the first thing Nixon did was to demand signed resignations of his entire government. "Eliminate everyone," he told John Ehrlichman, "*except George Bush. Bush will do anything for our cause.*"[4]

Other members of the Watergate team who were coordinated by Bush for the invasion of Cuba over a decade before were Frank Sturgis, E. Howard Hunt, Bernard Barker and Rafael "Chi Chi" Quintero. Quintero worked with CIA coordinator William F. Buckley, Jr. in a special assassination unit run under the cover of Pemex Oil Co. in Mexico in the early 1980s before Buckley's return to Beirut and his subsequent capture and torture to death by a radical Islamic group. The longtime CIA hitman has said publicly that if he ever told what he knew about

---

3   Theresa A, "Three Men and a Barge," *Common Cause*, March-April, 1990, and Frank Sturgis interview, *San Francisco Chronicle*, May 7, 1977, in which he stated that *"the reason we burglarized the Watergate was because Nixon was interested in stopping news leaking relating to the photos of our role in the assassination of President John Kennedy."*

4   Sidney Blumenthal, *Pledging Allegiance*.

Dallas and the Bay of Pigs *"it would be the biggest scandal ever to rock the nation."*

Bush claims he never worked for the CIA until he was appointed Director by President Ford in 1976. Of course, Bush has a company duty to deny being in the CIA. The CIA is a secret organization. No one ever admits to being a member.

The truth is that Bush has been a top CIA agent since before the 1961 invasion of Cuba, working with Felix Rodriguez and other anti-Castro Cubans. Bush may deny his work for the CIA in 1959, but there are records in the files of Rodriguez and others involved in the Bay of Pigs invasion of Cuba that expose Bush's role. The corporations would not put somebody in charge of all the state secrets held by the CIA unless he was experienced and well trained in the CIA.[5]

The initial reaction of Senator Frank Church, chair of the Senate Select Committee on Intelligence, to the firing of William Colby and the naming of Bush as CIA Director, was that it was part of attempts by Ford (a former member of the Warren Commission) to impede the Church Committee's investigation into CIA assassination plots, with which Colby was cooperating, but which Ford was trying to keep secret. Within days of Bush's advent as DCI, the hemorrhage ended.

Did Congress realize that Nixon and Bush had openly discussed killing JFK for stopping the air cover for the Bay of Pigs invasion of Cuba? Remember, Nixon taped virtually every discussion he had with anyone in his inner circle, including Bush. There is a photo of Bush reporting to Nixon in the White House in 1968. It will be interesting to see what they were talking about on that day, when the full 4000 hours are released.

---

5   Bush, in fact, did work directly with the anti-Castro Cuban groups in Miami before and after the Bay of Pigs invasion, using his company, Zapata Oil, as a corporate cover for his activities on behalf of the Agency. Records at the University of Miami, where the operations were based for several years, show that George Bush was present during this time period.

In his autobiography, *Looking Forward*, Bush describes some of his political adversaries in Texas, including Lyndon Johnson, John Connally, Ralph Yarborough, and Lloyd Bentsen, three of whom were in Dealey Plaza in Dallas in the motorcade which carried Kennedy to his death. Curiously, his only statement in the book concerning that event is "But now Johnson was President...."

Perhaps his seeming disinterest in Kennedy's killing can be traced to a single fact purposely left out of his glowing biography. Buried among the 98,755 pages of FBI documents released to the public in 1977 and 1978 as a result of Freedom of Information Act suits was a memo on November 29, 1963, one week after the assassination, from J. Edgar Hoover.

Written to the director of the State Department's Bureau of Intelligence and Research, Hoover described the briefing given to *"George Bush of the Central Intelligence Agency"* the day after the assassination, when Lee Harvey Oswald was interrogated about his connections to Cuban exiles and the CIA. Oswald's ties to the CIA and Naval Intelligence are virtually undisputed; the likelihood that Bush functioned on behalf of either of the two agencies is even greater, given his early service as a naval aviator and his family's close ties to the military-industrial complex.

The briefing was held, according to the FBI director, because the State Department feared that *"some misguided anti-Castro group might capitalize on the present situation and undertake an unauthorized raid against Cuba, believing that the assassination of President John F. Kennedy might herald a change in U.S. policy, which is not true."*

"The substance of the foregoing was furnished to Bush and Capt. William Edwards of the Defense Intelligence Agency on November 23 by Mr. W.T. Forsyth of this Bureau."

Bush himself described his CIA appointment by President Ford as a "real shocker." In his autobiography, Bush points out, *"I'd come to the CIA with some general knowledge of how it operated.* " His remark in the book that his "overseas experience as a businessman" helped qualify him for the appointment by President Nixon as ambassador to the United Nations could also refer to his experience as a CIA agent.

Bush's autobiography is vague about his activities in the early 1960s, when he was running the Houston-based Zapata Off-Shore Company. "Running an offshore oil company," he wrote, "would mean days spent over water; not only the Gulf of Mexico but oceans and seas the world over."[6]

The 1972 profile of Bush in *Current Biography* provides more details of those years: "Bush travelled throughout the world to sell Zapata's oil-drilling services. Under his direction it grew to be a multi-million-dollar concern, with operations in Latin America, the Caribbean, the Middle East, Japan, Australia, and Western Europe." According to Nicholas King's *George Bush: A Biography*, his company, Zapata Oil, was concentrating in the Caribbean and off South America in the early 1960s, which meshes with the available data on Bush's early CIA responsibilities. An agent will often adopt the cover of a businessman, while business people have also served as informants for the Agency, passing along information picked up on their travels.

Informed by reporter Joseph McBride in mid-1988 of the 11/29/1963 J. Edgar Hoover memorandum, the then-Vice-President's spokesman, Stephen Hart, asked, "Are you sure it's the same George Bush?" After talking to the Vice President, Hart quoted him as follows, "I was in Houston, Texas, at the time and involved in the independent oil-drilling business. And I was running for the Senate in late '63." "Must be another George Bush," added Hart.

McBride then asked him via Hart:

• Did you do any work with or for the CIA prior to the time you became its director?

---

6 George Bush with Victor Gold, *Looking Forward* (New York: Doubleday, 1987), p. 70.

- If so, what was the nature of your relationship with the agency, and how long did it last?
- Did you receive a briefing by a member of the FBI on anti-Castro Cuban activities in the aftermath of the assassination of President Kennedy?

Half an hour later, Hart called McBride to say he had not spoken to the Vice President, but would answer the questions himself. The answer to the first question was no, he said, and so he would skip number two.

To the third, he repeated Bush's answer above, but added that Bush had also said, "I don't have any idea what he's talking about."

However, when Bush's denial was read back to him, Hart said that he preferred not to be quoted directly, explaining, "It's a week old now, and I'm going off my notes."

When McBride reminded him that he wanted to quote Bush directly, Hart said, "I am a spokesman. However you want to write it, the answer is no" regarding Bush's alleged 1963 involvement with the CIA.

CIA spokesman Bill Devine told McBride, "This is the first time I've heard this," when asked about Bush's CIA involvement in the early 1960s. The next day Devine called McBride with the terse response, "I can neither confirm nor deny." When he was told what Hart had said, and asked whether he could check whether there had been another George Bush in the CIA, Devine responded, "Twenty-seven years ago? I doubt that very much. In any event, we just have a standard policy of not confirming that anyone is involved with the CIA."

Richard Helms, who was deputy director at the Agency in 1963, told McBride Bush's name in the memo "must have been some kind of misprint. I don't recall anyone by that name working for the agency.... He certainly never worked for me."

McBride attempted to locate William T. Forsyth, but learned that he was dead. Forsyth worked out of the Washington FBI headquarters and was best known for running the investigation of the Rev. Martin Luther King Jr. Efforts to locate Captain Edwards of the Defense Intelligence Agency were unsuccessful.

Bush's specific duties with the CIA in 1963 — whether he was an agent, or merely an "asset" — cannot be determined from Hoover's memo. However, one of McBride's sources, who worked with the Agency in the late 1950s and 1960s said of the Vice President, *"I know he was involved in the Caribbean. I know he was involved in the suppression of things after the Kennedy Assassination. There was a very definite worry that some Cuban groups were going to move against Castro and attempt to blame it on the CIA."*[7]

After McBride's article concerning Hoover's 1963 memo appeared in *Nation* magazine, the CIA evidently changed its mind. On July 19, 1988, Agency spokeswoman Sharon Basso told the Associated Press that the 1963 Hoover memo "apparently" referred not to Vice President George Bush but to George *William* Bush, who had worked in 1963 on the night watch at CIA headquarters, which "would have been the appropriate place to have received such an FBI report." Basso said *this* George Bush left the CIA in 1964 to work for the Defense Intelligence Agency.

Why did the Agency break with its longstanding policy of "neither confirm nor deny"? Basso said it believed "the record should be clarified." Another CIA official told the AP, "We put a lot of effort into this."

Hart of the VP's office told the same thing to Sarah Perl of the *Nation*.

Both Perl and McBride called the DIA, which confirmed that George William Bush had worked there between Feb. 1964 and July 1965, performing the same duties as a CIA civilian-grade government intelligence-research specialist, with the relatively low-level rank of GS-7.

Although the Agency claimed that whereabouts of this Bush

---

7   Joseph McBride, *Nation*, July 23, 1988, p. 37, 41-2

were unknown, McBride located him at 401 Cambridge Road, Alexandria, Virginia. A check of directories showed that a George W. Bush "emp US govt" lived at the Cambridge Road address in 1964. When McBride reached George William Bush, who was 49 at that time and worked for the Social Security Administration, Bush confirmed that he had worked for the CIA for about six months in 1963-64 as a coast and landing-beach analyst — not as a night watchman — in those years, with the rank of GS-5. He definitely did *not* receive the FBI briefing in 1963, he stated.

When McBride read him the Hoover memo about the FBI briefing, his response was, *"Is that the other George Bush?"*

While in the CIA, George William Bush said he had never received interagency briefings because he was "just a lowly researcher and analyst" and worked only with documents and photographs. He said he "knew neither one" of two people the memorandum mentions being briefed, William T. Forsyth of the FBI and Capt. William Edwards of the DIA. "So it wasn't me," he said.

George William Bush said he left the CIA because he was offered a job by the DIA at a higher grade and salary, and he stayed until joining the Social Security Administration in Jan. 1968. He professed he was "a little bit amazed, but not entirely surprised" that the CIA and the DIA divulged his employment with them. "I didn't know they were at liberty to release all this. It was certainly without advance notice," he said, adding that he had not known of the story in the *Nation* about George Bush's alleged 1963 ties with the CIA.

The Social Security Administration confirmed that *this* George Bush was currently employed in its Arlington, Virginia office, and verified other points in his story, particularly aspects of his life prior to working with the CIA. In addition, George William Bush repeated his story to Victor Navasky, editor of the *Nation,* reiterating that he was *not* the man referred to in the FBI memorandum.

Why would the CIA indicate that this man was the George

Bush in the Hoover memo without any attempt to locate him, and why would the media repeat the Agency's version without checking? Where was George Herbert Walker Bush on November 22 and 23, 1963. Was he working for the CIA then?

While the full extent of his role is vague, the newly discovered FBI document places Bush in Miami recruiting right-wing Cuban exiles for the invasion of Cuba.

Bush lived in Houston, Texas, hopping to Miami weekly. Bush spent 1960 and '61 recruiting Cubans in Miami for the invasion. That is how he met Felix Rodriguez, who became part of a special CIA shooter team which was coordinated out of a secret triangular-fire training base in Mexico maintained by the domestic counter-intelligence Division Five of the FBI.[8]

Felix Rodriguez was the Iran-Contra CIA agent who told the world in October 1986, that the CIA plane flown by Gene Hasenfus had crashed in Nicaragua. As soon as Rodriguez heard that the plane crashed, he called Samuel Watson, staff aide to his CIA supervisor, Donald Gregg, who was now national security adviser to the Vice President, Bush.

Bush has denied being in the contra loop, but investigators recently obtained copies of Oliver North's diary, which documents Bush's role as a CIA supervisor of the contra-supply network. Aiding the contras was President Reagan's major anti-communist thrust. In 1988 Bush told Congress he knew nothing about the illegal supply flights until late November 1986, yet North's diary shows Bush at the first planning meeting Aug. 6, 1985.

Bush's "official" log placed him somewhere else (see chapter 4). Such double sets of logs have long been used to hide

---

8   William Torbitt, "Nomenclature of an Assassination Cabal," also referred to as "the Torbitt Document." Reference from the case files of Bill Alcorn, special assistant Attorney General of Texas, concerning the murder by two such assassins in 1952 of 19-year-old Buddy Floyd, son of Jake Floyd, district judge in Alice, Texas, the actual target of the assassination.

Bush's real role in the CIA to provide "plausible deniability." The problem is, it failed because too many people, like North and Rodriguez, kept records that show Bush's role back to the 1961 invasion of Cuba.[9]

The discovery of the Hoover memo, stating that, *"Mr. George Bush of the Central Intelligence Agency"* had been briefed on November 23, 1963 about the reaction of anti-Castro Cuban exiles in Miami to the assassination of Kennedy, however, stirs speculation as to what Bush had been doing during this time.

It is believed by many that Bush was in Texas the day before, but, like Nixon and Hoover, he has denied it. It has been reported that Nixon and Hoover *were* in Dallas the night before at the ranch of Texas oil baron Colin J. "Clint" Murchison, Jr. A newspaper article described Nixon's stay at the Baker Hotel in Dallas, ostensibly for a Pepsi-Cola executives' convention. Retired Brig. Gen. Penn Jones reported that Murchison, Hoover and others met at Murchison's house in Dallas November 21, 1963.[10]

Within hours of Kennedy's death, a man identifying himself as "George H.W. Bush" telephoned the FBI's Houston office with information about a threat allegedly made against Kennedy by a young, right-wing Republican.

The FBI report concerning this call was made public in the late 1970s as a result of lawsuits under the Freedom of Information Act (FOIA). It stated that, "On November 22, 1963, Mr. George H.W. Bush, 5525 Briar, Houston, Texas, telephonically advised...that one James Parrott has been talking of killing the president when he comes to Houston."

According to Nixon's biography, his personal and political ties with the Bush family go back to 1946, when Nixon claims he read an ad placed in an L.A. newspaper by the Orange

---

9   *Washington Post*, January 10, 1990.

10   William Penn Jones, *Forgive My Grief*, Volumes 1-IV.

County Republican Party and a wealthy group of businessmen, led by Prescott Bush, the father of George Bush.

They wanted a young candidate to run for Congress. Nixon applied and won the job, becoming a mouthpiece for the Bush group, progressing to the U.S. Senate and in 1952 the vice presidency.[11]

In 1960, Vice President Nixon was scouring the world seeking the presidency. At his side was Prescott Bush. Congressman Gerald Ford was helping raise funds, as was George Bush.

It took Nixon eight more years to reach his goal. And the canny politician always remembered who helped him get there. So again it was payback time for George Bush. Nixon appointed him Chairman of the Republican National Committee, and later ambassador to China.

By 1976, Ford, who succeeded Nixon after Watergate, paid his due bill. He picked out a big job for his old crony, Bush: the CIA. But this time Bush would not be an underling. Now he would be head man.

---

11   Fletcher Prouty, *Freedom* Magazine, 1986.

CHAPTER 4

Company Man

George Bush is "the perfect yes man."

Larry Speakes, President Reagan's press secretary

"Neither James Schlesinger nor Stan Turner were very popular with the pros because both of them set out with antagonism to the CIA. Bush didn't."

A senior CIA analyst, quoted in the one paragraph devoted to George Bush as Director of the CIA in John Ranelagh's *The Agency*

Miles Copeland, the CIA operative who betrayed the Desert One hostage rescue operation in print several days before it was activated in April 1980, claimed that George Bush was the best director of the CIA, "He came in knowing he didn't know a damn thing about the CIA, but he did know how to judge people whose opinion he could trust, and he listened to them."[1]

In fact, no other candidate has been exposed to so many facets of the national security world. Bush has served as a congressman, ambassador to the United Nations, envoy to China, and director of the Central Intelligence Agency. As vice president, Bush headed National Security Council groups on crisis management, drug interdiction and terrorism.

In 1976 Bush became a Cabinet-level officer for the first time, as CIA director. For a year, Bush called the shots as

---

1   Miles Copeland interview, *Bangkok Post,* 1/19/86.

intelligence czar in the Ford Administration. What happened during that year? And what did Bush do as the CIA's top man?

His record, as profiled in 1988 by *The New York Times Sunday Magazine,* shows no distinguishable accomplishments, merely one prestigious position after another adding up to an impressive resume. Bush's days at CIA followed a predictable pattern: mind the store quietly, make no waves, ruffle no feathers, make friends not enemies — friends, who, when the time came, could be counted on to help him climb another rung on the ladder of unbounded ambition.

According to former aides and a high-ranking CIA official, Bush helped restore the CIA's damaged morale and re-establish ties with foreign intelligence agencies. He also effectively sheltered the Agency from Congressional scrutiny.

But in the process, Bush "virtually turned the store over" to the covert operatives and "dirty tricksters" he was supposedly bringing under rein. During Bush's tenure, the message to the intelligence community was clear: Bush would look the other way, ignoring improprieties necessary to get the job done.

Covert operators learned that the way to deal with Bush was to keep him "out of the loop" for information about operations that Congress might challenge. By the time he left in January 1977, Bush had also learned that "out of the loop" was a safe place to be, especially if one had presidential ambitions.

If the appointment of George Herbert Walker Bush as CIA director was not preordained, neither was it entirely accidental. As often happens in Washington, Bush's elevation to the country's top spymaster was typical Washington, a payoff, for the most part, of hard partisan politics.

As Gerald Ford prepared to run for re-election in late 1975, he was an incumbent with practically no record, facing plenty of obstacles. His pardon of Richard Nixon had turned into a political tar baby. Additionally House and Senate committees were revealing, on an almost daily basis, news of abuses by the CIA. White House political strategists had been counting on a public relations break from the sensational exposés swirling around the CIA. William Colby, Ford's director of central intelligence, had been lauded by Congressional investigators for his cooperation. But the result of Colby's efforts turned out to be an endless series of revelations: secret drug testing, spying on U.S. citizens, and plotting assassinations of foreign leaders.

Even when these events occurred under Democratic administrations, each revelation tainted Ford. Colby, a symbol of past abuses, would have to be replaced. Ford's aides sorted through a "final" list of possible successors to Colby, but they were unsure if any could sufficiently reassure both the public and Congress.

They approached Edward Bennett Williams, a prominent trial lawyer and longtime Democrat, who turned it down. They then decided to offer it to Elliott Richardson, whose reputation for independence had been enhanced by his resignation as attorney general during the Watergate scandal. Before Richardson could be offered the job, however, partisan politics intervened.

Ford, after all, needed to be nominated and Vice President Nelson Rockefeller was feared too liberal to carry a Ford ticket through the Republican convention with a strong right-wing challenge promised by Ronald Reagan. Ford needed a conservative running mate, but as soon as he settled on Robert Dole his advisers feared that George Bush, already miffed at having been passed up for the vice presidency when Rockefeller was selected, could be troublesome.

Only five months after Bush had arrived as chief of the U.S. Liaison Office in Beijing, some of his visitors began leaking word that his first year in China would probably be his last. He had expressed interest in Secretary of Commerce, but Ford worried that if Bush returned in such a prominent role in January 1976, he would be free to challenge Ford or take a shot at the vice presidency.

The Ford White House wanted a Democrat or an independent Republican as Director of Central Intelligence. If they gave Bush the job, he would be forced to bow out of the 1976 race, so they decided to offer Richardson, Commerce, and Bush, the CIA.

Bush was a sensible, if political, choice. He was a loyal Republican whose impressive dossier included membership in Skull and Bones, the prestigious secret society at Yale; a father who was a moderate Republican senator from Connecticut during the Eisenhower and Kennedy Administrations; two terms in the House of Representatives from Texas; an unsuccessful, but not embarrassing, campaign against Lloyd Bentsen for a U.S. Senate seat in 1970; a tour as ambassador to the United Nations, in which he encountered every imaginable foreign affairs issue; yeoman service as chair of the beleaguered Republican National Committee during the darkest hours of Nixon's term, and the stint in Beijing.

Only those who worked closely with Bush knew that in the U.N. job he had deferred alternately to the State Department and to his own staff. He loyally obeyed detailed instructions from Henry Kissinger as well. Similarly, insiders knew how completely irrelevant he had been to U.S.-China policy.

Despite Bush's public persona as a world statesman, until his job as director of the CIA he had actually been a messenger carrying out orders for the Nixon and Ford administrations.

Kissinger cabled Bush in Beijing with the offer of CIA director on November 1, 1975. Bush consulted his wife, Barbara, before accepting. Only two weeks earlier, Kissinger had been in Beijing to arrange for President Ford's December trip to China, but he hadn't mentioned the offer.

By the time Bush returned to Washington, key Republicans from the House and Senate had asked him to withdraw from consideration for vice president, to prevent any implication of politicizing the CIA.

As he prepared for confirmation hearings in mid-December, he began hearing from old friends that he had been "a damned fool to say yes" and give up his own political future. His Yale classmate and fellow Skull & Bones member, Thomas Ludlow "Lud" Ashley, a House Democrat at the time, asked Bush,

"What the fuck do you know about intelligence?"

"Ask me in six weeks," a confident Bush responded (not daring to mention that — based on our information — he'd been on the CIA payroll for at least 15 years).

At the end of January, Bush was confirmed by the Senate. As he moved into the CIA's Langley, Virginia, headquarters, he took control of the most inbred bureaucracy in government. Room 7D5607 was an unattractive, cramped, L-shaped office. It had a square sitting area with a column incongruously placed in the middle, a cramped alcove housing the director's desk, and picture windows overlooking a panorama of the Virginia woods nearby.

In his first months on the job, Bush focused on altering the Agency to satisfy Capitol Hill. Bush's central charge would be to control the House and Senate intelligence committees.

The more hostile of the two, the House Committee, chaired by New York Democrat Otis Pike, soon gave Bush an unexpected opportunity. On February 11 and 18, 1976, the Village Voice published a copy of the Pike Committee report, later acquired through CBS correspondent Daniel Schorr. The CIA argued that the report contained information that endangered U.S. agents and compromised the country's intelligence-gathering capability.

Overnight the political mood shifted from support of the CIA to questions about the motives of its critics. Bush took advantage of the shift.

As principal liaison to Capitol Hill, Bush initiated a relationship with key Democrats and Republicans on the Senate Intelligence Committee. According to its staff director, William Miller, Bush seemed cooperative and forthcoming, a "member of the club" who had regular access to the President.

According to former aides of Bush, although he regularly briefed the President, and had a permanent rotation in Ford's tennis foursome, he exercised less influence over President Ford than was assumed.

On February 18, 1976, the Ford White House caught the unsuspecting congressional committees by surprise. By issuing Executive Order 11905, "to establish policies to improve the quality of intelligence needed for national security [and] to clarify the authority and responsibilities of the intelligence departments and agencies," Ford preempted a statute whereby Congress could tell the Executive what to do. Ironically, although this reorganization of the intelligence community would become one of the hallmarks of his service as the Agency's director, Bush had nearly nothing to do with it. It had been worked out over the previous six months by two Ford advisers.

The Senate Intelligence Committee, sensing that it lacked public support for extending its inquiry, struck a secret arrangement with Bush and the CIA, according to two of the committee's senior staff members.

Rather than move to a new oversight process, there would be a break during which the committee would neither set specific reporting requirements nor pass legislation. Bush would share information with the committee, with both parties understanding that a more cooperative oversight relationship would evolve over time.

For Bush it was imperative to get the Agency back to business. The most pressing priority was to restore the confidence and morale of the thousands of agents who felt that their actions would be examined and criticized by Congress and the press.

Bush "took pride in the morale-building sessions...he considers this one of his real accomplishments. I find that a little strange," says his friend Lud Ashley, who spoke often with Bush about his experience as director.

As he settled into the CIA job, Bush continued his pep-rally approach to management. Bush's perception of his responsibility was to deliver information to the President, and not to implement policy or linger at the table as a decision maker.

He considered himself uninvolved in major foreign-policy decisions. For those around Ford, this helped Bush as a buffer with the Hill; he was the honest broker, not a player calling the shots.

While Bush had done little but accept instructions from Washington, he now sat at the Cabinet table. What he brought to the table was largely what his deputies pushed. There were few opportunities to exercise his own initiative, even if he desired. If Bush had been deferential and loyal to his staff in previous jobs, he became almost obedient to those he was overseeing in the new job.

With the lingering odor of past abuses stifling support for new adventures, Bush's year at the CIA was one in which covert operations intensified with greater secrecy than ever.

Some of the problems he'd inherited concerning covert operations lingered on. The Senate committee wanted to know more, for example, about what was going on in Angola, since the Senate had prohibited any financial support to Jonas Savimbi's rebel forces there.

Bush's greatest asset in carrying the Angola ball turned out to be his delicate balance of knowledge and ignorance.

In the beginning, he was able to honestly report that, to his knowledge at least, the Agency was limiting further U.S. covert involvement.

The CIA had narrowly averted an investigation the previous December, when Deputy Director for Operations William Nelson testified to the Senate Foreign Relations Committee that the Agency was sending arms to Angola, the opposite of what the CIA had claimed. Now, with Bush at the helm, the Agency reassured Congress that aid had indeed been cut off.

One continuing problem was the revelation of CIA manipulation of public opinion in this country. Case officers from the Lusaka, Zambia, station had planted propaganda in the U.S. press in late September 1975 that Soviets were in Angola advising government forces. In fact, there was no evidence for this claim, but the Agency continued planting disinformation about Cuban soldiers committing nonexistent atrocities. In February 1976, a

CIA-sponsored free-lance journalist reported falsely in the Washington Post that South Africans were not assisting Savimbi.

The CIA continued to deny to congressional committees that arms were still being shipped to the Angolan rebels when, in fact, they continued to be shipped, through allies in the region. As each detail about illegalities and improper aid was revealed, Bush first denied, then admitted the CIA wrongdoing, adding that he had just learned the news.

When Bush went to the Hill for closed-door briefings, he shared little he had learned about the Angolan situation, and then in generalities. Here, according to those who attended the briefings, he seemed sincere and cooperative. When necessary, Bush brought along aides who were familiar with the matter at hand. He soon found he was not easily second-guessed by his audiences on the Hill.

Offering committee members greater detail than before, and patiently listening to their advice, Bush restored a foreign policy of secret consensus between the administration and key Republicans and Democrats about containing Soviet and Cuban expansion in Southern Africa.

One by one, the elected officials bought into the plan. According to two senior government officials, limited actions in Angola were on again, justified to phase out the larger, earlier operations.

By spring, Bush felt he had the Agency on solid ground with the congressional oversight committees, but there was one lingering problem: alleviating resentment in Congress toward certain Agency personnel. Bush knew changes had to be made, but he decided to allow the bureaucracy to guide his appointments to the upper echelon. From the time of his confirmation, Bush relied principally on E. Henry Knoche, a CIA veteran who helped coordinate Colby's and Bush's responses to the congressional committees.

Bush "relied on Knoche because he knew the place," notes one old hand. Knoche was considered the "general manager of the store." Another career officer puts it differently. He says

Knoche knew "where the bodies were buried or half-buried."

Bush also turned to William Wells, a career covert operator who had graduated ahead of him at Yale, as deputy for operations. A month later, on Wells' recommendation, Bush appointed Theodore Shackley associate deputy director for operations. A third career covert operator, John Waller, became inspector general, responsible for monitoring internal improprieties.

Professionals in the ranks were split over the changes. Some, particularly analysts and post-Vietnam War in-house critics, thought the fox had won a long-term lease on the henhouse. Others, particularly those serving in operations, thought the correct message was being communicated: covert actions are specialty items. It takes specialists to run them; it takes specialists to investigate them.

Throughout the fall of 1975 and spring of 1976, news stories about a new strain of intelligence abuses surfaced on Capitol Hill. This time committed not by the CIA, but by intelligence agencies of regimes friendly to the United States. A standard feature of the internal-security apparatus of these allies, Argentina, Chile, Iran, Israel, the Philippines, South Africa, South Korea, and Taiwan had been harassment of opposition figures, both domestically and abroad. Some of these countries' intelligence operatives, especially the Koreans, were courting members of Congress with campaign contributions, bribes, and favors ranging from ersatz antiques to party girls.

A growing number in the post-Watergate Democratic Congress found this particularly unattractive. They felt continued unrestrained activities of these foreign intelligence services threatened to undermine congressional and public confidence in the agency again.

To worsen matters, reports had come to Bush about preparations by Cuban-American veterans of the CIA's Miami station, including some who remained on the informant payroll to attack pro-Castro targets. Previously viewed as freedom fighters, these Cuban-Americans had become reckless terrorists, over whom the CIA had lost all control.

In June, four Cuban-American organizations joined together to form CORU, or the Command of United Revolutionary Organizations.

CORU was formed to build political support for overthrowing Castro, and its members began working directly with the intelligence agencies of the right-wing regimes in Chile, Paraguay and Nicaragua. After a CORU meeting at Bonao, a mountain resort in the Dominican Republic, consistent reports of planned bombings and political assassinations filtered back to the CIA.

Within six weeks, bombs exploded at the Cuban United Nations mission in New York, and at four other locations in the hemisphere. The first terrorist war in the Americas was under way, and it was being waged by agents trained and paid by the CIA.

The CIA had never restrained "friendly" intelligence agencies and was reluctant to preempt Cuban-America anti-Castro activity. The acts, including illegal ones, were occurring mostly outside the United States. Even when these acts were plotted inside the United States, they were officially the FBI's responsibility.

Unless the Agency continued to look the other way, it would open a Pandora's box of congressional investigation. Hoping to avoid years of additional inquiry, Bush's aides kept him as free of "irrelevant details," thus maximizing his ability to deny there was a problem. Reports of Cuban-American activity were handled routinely within the bureaucracy below, and rogue operations were seldom reined in. There were, however, exceptions to this.

In February 1976, the CIA blew the whistle on Orlando Bosch, a Miami pediatrician and anti-Castro organizer. Bosch was detained by Costa Rican police for plotting to assassinate Henry Kissinger, who had been conducting negotiations to improve relations with Cuba.

The CIA also intervened when officials learned the Chilean Intelligence Service (DINA) was planning to use Cuban ex-CIA agents to assassinate Chilean exiles in Portugal and France through a regional counter-terrorist organization known as Operation Condor.

Headed by Chile, Operation Condor included agents from Argentina, Bolivia, Paraguay, Brazil and Uruguay dedicated to tracking down "subversives" throughout the hemisphere. The details of the plot were passed to the CIA's intelligence liaisons in Portugal and France, and they squelched it.

In these cases, Bush's CIA proved capable of averting attacks planned by its friends. Unfortunately for targets of similar plots, the Agency did not develop any way of dealing with such terrorist threats. On June 16, 1976, U.S. Ambassador to Lebanon Francis E. Meloy, Jr., his driver, and the embassy's economic counselor were assassinated on their way to a meeting with Lebanese president-elect Elias Sarkis. President Ford convened an emergency meeting to focus on the potential danger to other Americans in Lebanon.

The crisis group — Ford, Bush, Kissinger, National Security Adviser Brent Scowcroft, Deputy Defense Secretary William Clements, Jr., and Chairman of the Joint Chiefs of Staff George Brown — convened four times in four days.

On this occasion, Bush moved beyond information-provider, feeling that the murder meant a "new, more dangerous level of terrorist activity in Beirut." This would warrant ordering Americans to evacuate, a move Kissinger opposed. Ford agreed with Bush: a Navy task force moved in and evacuated 166 people.

Bush was thrilled with his expanded role. He went back to the Agency, anxious to follow through with more information. For the first time in his career he was really a center-stage actor on a par with Kissinger. Bush wanted to know what the Agency could do to react to this new terrorist threat.

The analytical side of the CIA had little that could help Bush. The National Security Agency had overheard millions of conversations from special listening posts and satellites around the world, and was beginning to process this through its new, advanced Cray computers. But the results were largely useless, according to a ranking intelligence official, because Bush and his predecessors had ignored warnings that the expanded technological take of signals intercepted would not be processed without more money.

Bush had been granted the responsibility for the first time in CIA history to control the budgets of all intelligence agencies. There was virtually nothing the Agency analysts could do to assess, or help combat, the terrorists in Lebanon. So Bush turned to the clandestine operators who routinely collect human intelligence abroad.

Within the clandestine service side of the Agency, the Meloy assassination raised serious questions. Most intelligence from Lebanon came from three sources: Mossad, Israel's intelligence service; SAVAK, Iran's intelligence service; and a limited group of Lebanese Phalangists and assorted rightists taken out of the Athens CIA station by Richard Welch.

In general, the ability to keep up files on opposition parties, dissidents, and expatriate political factions in any country depends on the cooperation of the host government. With Welch's murder the previous December, the Agency had become more dependent on information from Israel and Iran.

U.S. intelligence officials felt they needed to reciprocate to get cooperation. The Korean CIA was interested in Korean dissidents in the United States; SAVAK wanted to know the movements of the Shah's opposition; Mossad wanted information on Palestinian political maneuvers in Washington; the Philippines secret police needed reports on anti-Marcos forces; and so forth.

As a result of legislation and the intelligence reforms of the previous year, though, the CIA was banned from domestic surveillance, including watching foreign opposition movements based in the United States. In short, the CIA had less and less to share with its counterparts abroad.

The information Bush wanted could be obtained, the CIA's

clandestine operators assured him, if Bush made it clear that the CIA would not crack down on "cooperative" intelligence agency activities and report their plans to the FBI. At that point, according to a still-active CIA official, Bush made a tactical judgment, one of the few of his career. He wanted to concentrate on collecting more information on terrorist activities around the world. To get it, the CIA had to cooperate with friendly foreign agencies in the United States. No further pressure would be brought on rogue operations of "cooperative" intelligence agencies. He would try to find ways to help them rather than to curtail their activities.

A new round of damaging self-examination was not a pleasant prospect for Bush. He had recently spoken publicly about the Agency's success in overcoming its adversarial relationship with Congress. "How we can ferret out corruption has given way to the more serious question of how we can get better intelligence," Bush said on ABC's Issues and Answers. Oversight, Bush said, was no longer to see if "everybody at the CIA is a bunch of crooks," but to improve the job the intelligence agencies were doing. Bush dreaded having to watch the adversarial relationship reemerge. Any indication that the CIA was operating "off the books" would surely spawn precisely that reaction.

Bush's tenure at the CIA would end at President Carter's inauguration, but until the end, Attorney General Levi pursued criminal cases against CIA officials and demanded CIA documents. Most disturbing to the Agency was the accumulated evidence in a possible prosecution of former CIA Director Richard Helms for lying to Congress about the Agency's involvement in the overthrow of Chilean President Salvador Allende.

Although the CIA's own three-person team had recommended in December 1974 that Helms be prosecuted, the Agency dragged its heels until after Bush took office. But in March 1976, former Ambassador to Chile Edward Korry forwarded a letter to Levi directly contradicting what Helms and several other witnesses told the Senate Intelligence Committee.

Helms' lawyer, Edward Bennett Williams, used his position on the President's Foreign Intelligence Advisory Board to argue against an indictment, according to a knowledgeable official. To indict Helms would be unfair, Williams claimed, because his client had not wanted to mislead or lie to the committee but only to honor his oath to keep the CIA's secrets. Bush interceded to argue that the outgoing administration should drop the Helms case rather than leave him to the mercy of the new Democratic administration.

In this case, as in others, Bush found himself at odds with the Justice Department. He was also unhappy when the department, despite the CIA's request, declined for the second time to prosecute Washington Post reporter Bob Woodward, according to an official in the department at that time. On December 12, 1976, Woodward had published the first account of CIA electronic surveillance of government representatives from Micronesia. Bush's job was to protect the CIA's sources and methods. He believed Woodward and his sources had violated the Signals Intelligence Act, which makes it a felony to "knowingly and willfully" publish "in any manner prejudicial to the safety or interest of the United States" any classified information concerning at the CIA codes, ciphers, communications intelligence activities, or equipment used in cryptographic or communications intelligence.

When Bush had arrived at the CIA, a series of cases designed to find and punish reporters and their sources was being pushed forward by Kissinger, former Secretary of Defense Schlesinger, and National Security Adviser Scowcroft. These men, despite reservations of outgoing Director William Colby, had urged Attorney General Edward Levi to prosecute four journalists New York Times reporters Seymour Hersh and Nicholas Horrock, Woodward, and Tad Szulc.

But Levi and his staff, along with White House lawyers and political staffers, were reluctant to prosecute. They had serious doubts that the Signals Intelligence Act applied to journalists.

They also worried that the political climate, still heated from Watergate and the intelligence scandals, would make prosecution look like an attempt either to intimidate or to punish one of the journalists who had uncovered Watergate.

Levi asked Bush to release sufficient sensitive information concerning the published revelations on Micronesia to convince a jury that their publication had damaged national security. Bush balked, the stakes were too great for the CIA to confirm its role. As he had before, Levi said he would not go further without it.

At the end of December, Levi wrote Bush insisting that the CIA declassify and release the evidence about Helms and Chile that the prosecutors needed, or explain why it was being withheld. Inexplicable holes in documents were unacceptable. Levi cited "the President's stated position on this matter" in calling for prompt release of the missing materials. His staff made it clear to Bush's aides that they thought the CIA's attitude "casual" and "cavalier" and that the Agency was, in effect, obstructing the investigation, according to former aides to both Bush and Levi.

Levi's irritation grew as prosecutors said the Helms documents had been provided only reluctantly, and were poor-quality copies. Even in the Letelier murder investigation, in which the agreement between Levi and Bush had been most explicit, little useful material had been included in the tons of cables and peripheral reports passed to the FBI.

Documents obtained by FAIR, released through the Freedom of Information Act (FOIA), show that Bush, tried to bottle up a news story that exposed the apparent duplicity of another former CIA chief, Helms.

The story, broken on Oct. 1, 1976, by David Martin (now CBS Pentagon correspondent, then with Associated Press) revealed that Helms had given misleading testimony to the Warren Commission investigating the assassination of John Kennedy. Helms testified that the CIA had not "even contemplated" making contact with Lee Harvey Oswald, the presumed assassin.

Through the FOIA, Martin obtained CIA memos showing that in 1960 the agency "showed intelligence interest" in Oswald and "discussed...the laying on of interviews" with him.

When Bush saw the AP story in the Washington Star, he asked for an internal CIA review to verify the story (it was true) and if it would "cause problems for Helms." Helms had lied to a Senate committee about the CIA's role in subverting Chilean democracy and would later be convicted of contempt of Congress.

After investigating, Bush assistant Seymour Bolten reported the exposure of Helms' false testimony to the Warren Commission would probably cause Helms "some anxious moments," though not "any additional legal problems." But Bush was assured that a "slightly better" story had resulted from an Agency phone call to AP protesting that Martin's story was "sloppy." Additionally, Bush was told that an unnamed journalist had "advised his editors...not to run the AP story."

Bolten complained to Bush: "This is another example where material provided to the press and public in response to an FOIA request is exploited mischievously and is distorted to make headlines." One might more accurately describe it as an occasion where Bush's CIA pressured one news outlet to back away from an accurate story while using a connection in the press corps to suppress it in another.

Stung by revelations in the '70s about the CIA's hiring of journalists as spies, the Agency drafted regulations to prevent such practices. Researcher Robert Gardner obtained a copy of CIA policy "relations with Journalists and Staff of US News Media Organizations" and found that it contains loopholes big enough to drive truckloads of contra aid through.

The rules prohibit "relationships" with journalists accredited by U.S. media outlets, or the use of these outlets' names for intelligence purposes. The policy does not prohibit the hiring of freelance journalists, and it allows the CIA to recruit "non-journalist staff employees" (librarians, sound technicians and camerapersons?) of media outlets if authorization is given by senior media management.

According to documents recently released under the Freedom of Information Act, debate continued through phone calls and meetings until Levi and Bush agreed to let the President resolve the dispute. On January 17, three days before Carter's inauguration, they discussed the case in Brent Scowcroft's office. Levi, scheduled to appear before the Supreme Court later that day, was dressed in a morning suit, white tie and tails. He argued that if there was to be a prosecution there must be evidence that showed damage to national security.

Bush argued to the contrary; let the Justice Department make do with what information the CIA was willing to provide — a handful of older classified documents. These would do no damage if introduced into the court record. That was a good way to lose the case, Levi pointed out. Since they would do no damage if released, it was difficult to argue that they required classification to protect national security. To win meant showing damage and thus creating the damage.

So let the case be lost, Bush insisted. The psychological and financial trauma of being prosecuted would be punishment enough for Moore. They could decide later on what specific evidence would be used. Bush was adamant that no agent's name be compromised to help the prosecution. Even the non-sensitive names in the phone books opened those individuals to recruitment by the KGB, Bush said.

Once more, Levi launched into a lecture about constitutional safeguards. Defendants must learn the nature of the accusations (and thus the evidence) against them, just as they have the right to be confronted by witnesses against them. The CIA's continuing refusal to turn over materials the Justice Department needed "smacked of a Watergate cover-up" Levi told Bush.

These words hit hard, and the memories of his tenure at the Republican National Committee rushed into his mind. Bush's patience gave way. "We'll be taking it to the President in a few minutes," he said, his voice rising. "Why don't you tell him that in just those words?" These events were not "Nixonian," he added.

Eventually, Moore was prosecuted under Levi's terms. But Bush succeeded in stalling, if not in actually preventing the prosecutions of those associated with the CIA's role in Chile, the Wilson affair, and the assassination of Orlando Letelier.

Eventually, these cases would be acted upon more vigorously by Jimmy Carter's director of central intelligence, Stansfield Turner. When Turner began his own internal investigations, however, he would find Bush's closest aides most resistant.

A decade later, Bush included a most curious version of the Moore story in his autobiography. There, he described the case as his "biggest fight to protect CIA sources." In Bush's account, his angry objection to the Watergate reference intimidated Levi, causing him to cave in.

The author of Bush's biography, Victor Gold, says that the emphasis on the Moore case was his own choice, an editorial decision to liven up the book. Gold acknowledges that he had never heard about Bush's role in the more important cases: Helms, Wilson, and Letelier. Bush's spokesman, Steven Hart, says he cannot speak about those cases: "Before my time. Only the Vice President knows the answers." But Bush has repeatedly refused to be interviewed about his days as CIA director, emphasizing his oath to protect "methods and sources."

Interviews with former aides and current officials, as well as a careful examination of the record, suggests that Bush played the role of a cheerleader and a front man not knowing, or wanting to know of certain operations. He ignored repeated signals that rogue, "off-the-books" operations by former agents were out of control.

Bush was even more paralyzed in dealing with other countries' intelligence agencies, which were harassing, wiretapping, beating, kidnapping and intimidating their exile populations in the United States. In 1976, after Bush decided not to restrain "cooperative" foreign intelligence agencies, rogue operators became involved in blowing up an airliner, assassinating a former Chilean diplomat in Washington, attempting assassinations here and abroad, and smuggling arms.

Whether Bush was fully aware of the details, this set the tenor for the Iran-Contra scandal. Although accounts vary, this much is clear: Bush failed to conduct prudent internal inquiries, failed to purge the CIA of rogue connections, and failed to halt such behavior in policy statements.

For Bush, ignoring the problem of Manuel Antonio Noriega was normal procedure, dating to his days as CIA Director. Just three months after Bush moved in to his office at Langley, he was informed that the Army was investigating Noriega's activities. The details could embarrass the Ford administration and cause long-term political damage to the GOP, Precisely what Bush had been hired to prevent. The last thing Bush wanted to hear in his morning briefings was that one of his two-bit intelligence satraps from Panama was buying intelligence intercepts from U.S. military agents while he was on Bush's Agency payroll.

The case of the "Singing Sergeants," code-named "Canton Song," involved Noriega's purchase of reel-to-reel audiotapes from the Army's 470th Military Intelligence Group, which conducted high-tech wiretaps throughout the region under orders from the Defense Intelligence Agency.

The DIA had ordered the 470th specifically to tap Panamanian officials involved in negotiations over the Canal treaties. Former California Governor Ronald Reagan was already gaining ground in the Presidential primaries by denouncing Ford for giving away "our Panama canal." Public release of the "Canton Song" report would have damaged Ford's campaign.

It seems that Noriega, who was on the DIA payroll at the time, had discovered the surveillance. Instead of exposing the operation he allowed it to continue, and purchased some of the tapes for his boss, Panamanian strongman Omar Torrijos. The chief of the National Security Agency who was in charge of international electronic surveillance, Lew Allen, Jr., was intent on prosecuting the traitors, but Bush balked, saying he lacked authority and insisting that this was an Army matter.

The embarrassed Army decided to keep the scandal under wraps. Meanwhile, the CIA learned that Noriega had sold the sensitive intelligence which may have included wiretaps on Cuban and other leaders in the region to the Cuban DGI (Castro's intelligence service) which was also paying Noriega. Bush not only refused to punish the officers or Noriega, he continued to pay Noriega $110,000 a year.

Bush realized, however, that paying Noriega didn't necessarily mean that he was "bought." New intelligence in the fall linked Noriega to three bombings of American property and civilians in the Canal Zone. Noriega later claimed he'd been ordered to stir things up by Torrijos, who was angry over the Ford administration's delays in treaty negotiations.

In his final month as director, Bush confronted Noriega about his role in the bombings and "Canton Song," even though his efforts to "control the hemorrhaging" at the CIA had failed to prevent Ford from losing to Carter. Neither Ford nor Carter wanted any trouble during the transition, however, so Bush was constrained.

In 1988, Bush denied that he had ever met Noriega. Later he remembered the meeting, but not any details. His three lunch guests, however, have better memories. One of them insisted this was third meeting between the two men.[2]

On December 8, Bush arrived without an entourage for lunch at the elegant stone residence of Nicolas Gonzalez Revilla, the Panamanian ambassador in Washington. Noriega was waiting with the ambassador and Panamanian Foreign Minister

---

2   FOIA release: 470th Military Intelligence Group Information Report, Jan. 5, 1977. The Army's report on Noriega's trip to Washington referred to it as "unrevealed official business." The report also said he was traveling with a close associate, Whitgreen. Carlos Whitgreen was later indicted in Miami for arms trafficking.

Aquilino Boyd.[3] The contrast between the two intelligence chiefs was striking; the tall and refined New England-raised Brahmin towered, both literally and figuratively, over the five foot, five inch Noriega — a mean-streets mestizo — the bastard son of his father's domestic.

Acting as interpreter, Boyd sat next to Bush, across from Noriega, while Noriega stiffly repeated denials of Panamanian involvement in the bombings. According to Noriega, U.S. Ambassador Jordan, who had conveyed the charges, refused to provide proof, making it difficult for him and Foreign Minister Boyd to answer the accusations.

Bush remained laconic, saying only, "I'm listening. I'm listening."

It became obvious that Noriega's primary concern was to identify the Agency's source when he asked Bush, "Did you get the information from general McAuliffe [commander-in-chief of Southcom] or did you get it from the agent the CIA has planted inside the National Guard?"

Bush answered through Boyd, "We got the information from our man in the field."[4] Bush knew that Noriega was aware of the U.S. eavesdropping operations, but was Noriega aware that Bush knew? Up to that point, the CIA and Southcom had concealed their detection of "Canton Song"; now Noriega was announcing he knew the Agency had penetrated the National Guard and implying he knew the agent's identity. Bush was confirming the penetration, and the Agency's role avoiding

---

3   Years before, at the urging of Noriega's elder half-brother Luis Carlos, who worked as a clerk in the Foreign Ministry, Boyd, the minister, had agreed to authenticate a falsified birth certificate for Manuel Antonio, permitting him to attend the military academy in Peru. Russell Bowen, who has lived and worked extensively in Peru since the late 1940s, recalls having the young Panamanian cadet pointed out to him as an Agency "asset" during this time period by the U.S. Ambassador.

4   John Dinges, *Our Man in Panama* (New York: Random House, 1990), p. 88.

mention of the 470th's, but added nothing to help Noriega pinpoint the source.

Bush has never commented publicly about that meeting or any dealings with Noriega while he headed the CIA. During that period, however, he had several opportunities to review those dealings. At about the same time that he had been briefed on the Army's "Canton Song" investigation the previous April, Bush received the Justice Department's intelligence on its narcotics investigation known as the DeFeo report, which documented the government's unsuccessfully efforts to prosecute Noriega in 1971 and 1972.

The report is still highly classified, but in it is described at least one of the nebulous plans to assassinate Noriega and Torrijos. That plan was proposed by DEA agents Phillip Smith and William Durkin.

The other assassination plan which both the Reagan and Bush administrations have concealed from the American public, was put together by Green Beret Lt. Col. James "Bo" Gritz. As commander of Special Forces in Panama from 1974-76, Lt. Col. Gritz assembled a team to "terminate with extreme prejudice" Noriega.

Among the reasons cited by Gritz to eliminate Noriega were his role in cocaine smuggling, his collaboration with Fidel Castro, and numerous acts of sabotage against U.S. equipment and facilities in the Canal Zone.

As Gritz has recounted in two books and two documentary videos, Gen. Harold R. Aaron, Deputy Director of the Defense Intelligence Agency, met Gritz at Ft. Gulick in early 1976 to order him not to harm Noriega, since he was regarded to have "immense value" to Bush.[5]

Bush had certainly been briefed about Noriega's long-term relationship with the Agency, which had burst into full bloom

---

5   James "Bo" Gritz, *Called to Serve* (Sandy Valley, Nev.: Lazarus Publishing, 1991), p. 181.

after he became head of G-2 (military intelligence) in 1970. His CIA file described his help on the release of a captured Panamanian ship captain from Cuba, and his valuable intelligence on Torrijo's visit to the island as Bush eased into his office at Langley. Bush apparently had his own reasons for not taking Noriega to task over the bombings. According to Ambassador Jordan, "Bush listened courteously, never said what he really thought, and moved on to other matters. He was telling the Panamanians as subtly as he could, 'Let's drop this subject as long as it does not happen again.'"

Whatever well-justified anxiety George Bush might have had about Noriega's involvement in drugs, espionage and terrorism, his only voiced concern was "Is Torrijos a Communist?" Boyd assured him that was not the case.

A few days later Boyd received a package from Bush (sent by special messenger from CIA headquarters) containing a photo of a smiling Bush inscribed, "To Aquilino Boyd, With friendship and much respect, George." Noriega received an even warmer message of support from the Agency: he spent the rest of his visit to Washington as the house guest of Vernon Walters, Bush's deputy director.[6]

Bush now claims that as vice president he was kept in the dark about such important Reagan administration initiatives as trading arms to Iran for hostages and illegally funding the Nicaraguan contras. He has claimed that he first learned details of the scandal from Senator David Durenberger in December 1986 one month after the rest of the country found out about it in a televised press conference held by then-Attorney General Edwin Meese.

How could he have missed the unfolding disaster? "I was at the Army-Navy football game," Bush says of one key meeting where the policy was discussed. He also has no recollection of a second meeting at which Secretary of State George Schultz and

6   Dinges, p.90.

Secretary of Defense Caspar Weinberger argued vehemently against selling missiles to Iran. His staff suggests that he may have taken a washroom break.

When CBS anchorman Dan Rather questioned Bush about his lame responses in their television confrontation in January 1988, Bush insisted that he had been "out of the loop" on Iran policy and contra funding. "Uh, may I explain 'out of the loop?'" the Vice President added. "No operational role."

That was a curious thing to say, because high-level officials are not expected to have day-to-day operational involvement. But "out of the loop" in terms of knowledge about the policy? As chief of the National Security Council's Crisis Management team since 1981, and as vice president, Bush was privy to the same information provided to the President.

With Bush's record as background, though, his explanation is understandable. Bush has been on the scene of the nation's biggest scandals, from the Bay of Pigs to the assassination of John Kennedy to Watergate to Iran-Contra, and he is one of the few survivors. His unique combination of engagement and ignorance helped him navigate treacherous waters throughout his career.

When the Democrats began taunting "Where was George?" at their convention in July 1988, it was a signal that this strange record of uninvolved involvement, including his relationship with the national security world, had become a campaign issue.

For those who have worked closely with Bush, it seemed a silly taunt. His colleagues in the intelligence community almost describe Bush as a straight-shooting supervisor dedicated, honest, and loyal. But even his stoutest supporters admit, if pressed, that Bush is also deferential.

During the Nixon and Ford administrations, he delegated virtually every aspect of major decisions to career professionals. He also learned how to insulate himself from the fallout when disaster struck.

A review of the voluminous investigative record of the Iran-contra scandal demonstrates that there were only eight individuals, of hundreds involved, who were actually "in the loop" of detailed information about both the arms-for-hostages deal with Iran and funding for the Nicaraguan contras.

One, William Casey of the CIA, is dead. Five of the others, Robert McFarlane, John Poindexter, Oliver North, Richard Secord and Albert Hakim, have pleaded guilty or been indicted for their involvement in the loop. One left office on January 20, 1989.

The last, George Bush, took office on that day.

CHAPTER 5

An Election Held Hostage

"Espionage in a political campaign is not a criminal act."

Ronald Reagan

"Was I ever in Paris in 1980? Definitively, definitely no."

That's how George Bush reacted on May 3, 1991, when questioned whether he had attended an October 1980 meeting in Paris with Iranian officials to delay the release of the 52 American hostages held in Iran. The 52 were released on the day Ronald Reagan was inaugurated in January 1981. Ever since former Carter National Security aide Gary Sick published an Op Ed piece in *The New York Times* in April 1991 that quoted three sources saying they saw Bush at a Paris meeting, Congressional investigators and journalists have been trying to establish the President's comings and goings for the so-called "Lost Weekend" of October 18 through 20.

In 1990, Richard Brenneke, a self-professed agent, was tried in Portland, Oregon, for perjury after stating under oath that he knew Reagan/Bush campaign officials had negotiated a secret deal with the Iranians to keep the Americans hostage until after the 1980 election.

Brenneke has also said he delivered arms to the Ayatollah in the early 1980s. At Brenneke's trial, two Secret Service agents testified that they could not definitively, or even with a high degree of confidence, say where Bush was on October 19 because they kept no paperwork on that day.

At the same trial, Donald Gregg, currently U.S. Ambassador to South Korea and allegedly at the Paris meeting, testified he had spent the whole weekend with his family at Bethany Beach, Delaware. As proof, Gregg provided photographs of himself and his family on a sunny beach. However, weather reports for that weekend from the Indian River weather station 10 miles from Bethany Beach say the sky was overcast throughout the 18th and 19th of October. Brenneke was acquitted.[1]

The charges had arisen as a result of Brenneke's testimony in a federal court that George Bush was among the U.S. emissaries cutting a deal in Paris in October 1980 with representatives of the Khomeini regime to delay the release of the American hostages until after the elections. Brenneke testified in Denver Federal Court in 1988 while appearing as a character witness at the sentencing of Heinrich Rupp, a former Luftwaffe pilot and gold dealer convicted of bank fraud involving the Bank of Aurora in Aurora, Colorado. He claimed that Rupp was a CIA contract agent who had worked with Air America in Southeast Asia, insisting that Rupp's illicit banking activities were sanctioned by the CIA, a charge that the Agency denies. As a result Rupp's sentence was reduced from 40 years to two years.

Two years later the U.S. Government, charged Brenneke with making "false statements." After it was demonstrated that the prosecution's star witness, Donald Gregg, was lying when he claimed to have been at the Maryland seashore during October 19-21, 1980, rather than in Paris as Brenneke had charged, the jury acquitted Brenneke on all five counts.

Stephen Pizzo, co-author of *Inside Job: The Looting of America's Savings and Loans*, found further corroboration for Brenneke's story when he discovered a telex to an associate of Rupp's which links Bush to the Paris meeting and supports Pizzo's contention of CIA complicity in the growing S & L scandal. The telex was found amid the files of Bank of Aurora,

---

1   John Palmer Jr. in *The Oregonian*, April 25, 1990.

sent from Worldwide Commerce Exchange in Geneva, Switzerland to Rupp, dated January 24, 1985. The telex concerns the purchase of Swiss francs, with payments to be made to an account held by Rupp in Switzerland — payments "addressed to your bank officer, Mr. Wachs."

That name, Wachs, surfaced in 1988 when Doyle McManus of the *Los Angeles Times* Washington office, while preparing a story on the October Surprise, checked the reservation log at the Raphael Hotel in Paris, where the meeting with the Iranians is said to have taken place. McManus found a reservation for a "BUSH," made on September 28, 1980, together with a second for a "WACHS." What made this discovery so remarkable was that the hotel's management had told a reporter from *Der Spiegel* who had checked in late 1988 that it had no records of the September-October 1980 period.

S & L-October Surprise links are corroborated by another person who Barbara Honegger, author of *October Surprise*, helped to arrange the 1980 meeting with Iranian officials. Kenneth Qualls was the former lead pilot for Phoenix-based American Continental Corp., formerly headed by Charles Keating. After 1980, Qualls was the manager of flight-crew operations for Tiger Air charter, a CIA proprietary. He is also the personal pilot of former President Gerald Ford and T. Grojean, president of Flying Tiger Airlines.

Qualls has been linked to Heinrich Rupp by an internal message dated October 14, 1980, four days before the alleged meeting in Paris. The memo mentions a flight plan prepared by Tiger Air and requested by Rupp.

According to available records, Bush's whereabouts cannot be documented from Saturday evening October 18 until the following night, when he appeared at the Zionist Organization of America dinner in Washington, D.C. On April 22, 1991 a reporter at Detroit's WXYZ-TV asked Vice-President Dan Quayle if he could provide information about the 22 apparently unaccounted-for hours in Bush's schedule.

As a vice-presidential candidate, Bush was accorded Secret Service protection, so there normally would be an official record. Quayle promised to fill in the blanks for the viewer's stations. The next day, according to Alan Upchurch, executive producer of WXYZ News, the VP's office phoned to say that Bush had spent that Sunday at home, without a Secret Service escort, so there are no written records.[2]

In fact, four separate Secret Service accounts of Bush's whereabouts during the missing 22 hours have been published. With no verifiable schedule for Bush's Lost Weekend, the following chronology shows where Bush certainly was, and supports speculation he might have dashed away to a meeting in Paris.

Saturday, October 18, 1980: Bush visited two New Jersey towns, Elizabeth and Westfield, before moving to Philadelphia. After giving a speech at Widener University in Chester, Pennsylvania, he left at 9 p.m. for Washington, D.C. He was not seen again in public until seven the next evening. But the manager of the Howard Johnson motel in Chester, where Bush rented a room Saturday, told the Portland *Oregonian* in 1988 that Bush checked out at about 11 p.m. Stephen Hart, Bush's spokesperson at the time, told the paper that Bush went to Philadelphia and caught a plane to Andrews Air Force base outside of Washington, D.C. From there he went directly to his home in the capital. Secret Service reports, on the other hand, indicate that Bush flew to Washington National Airport that night, arriving at 9:25, 25 minutes after leaving Widener.

Sunday, October 19, 1980: Republican presidential campaign workers, asked in 1988 for an account of Bush's activities, said the candidate left Philadelphia and went to the Chevy Chase Country Club in Maryland, where he spent the remainder of Saturday evening, Sunday morning, and all Sunday afternoon. This is backed up by Secret Service reports produced for the Richard Brenneke perjury trial that say Bush was at the club

---

2   Joel Bleifuss, *In These Times*.

Sunday with unknown parties. The FBI investigated this and reported that no one at the country club could substantiate Bush's presence. A club representative said Bush was not a member of the club.

On May 8, 1991, *The Wall Street Journal's* Gordon Crovitz reported that another Secret Service account of the "Lost Weekend" outlined Bush's day this way: "Sunday, Oct. 19, Washington, D.C. (Lunch with Supreme Court Justice Potter Stewart and Mrs. Stewart)." This story was provided to the Government Accounting Office a few months ago. It, too, cannot be verified: Justice Stewart is dead, and his wife suffers from chronic memory loss. This version was confirmed last month by press secretary Marlin Fitzwater, who sketched Bush's itinerary to the *St. Louis Post-Dispatch*.

When approached by the *Village Voice* for Bush's itinerary for October 19, the White House media relations office denied one existed, adding, "We have nothing going that far back." A week later, the press office reversed itself, saying there was a schedule but that the only thing it showed for Sunday was the 7 p.m. speech to the Zionist Organization of America.

Jerry Saper of the *Washington Times* offered yet another version, "The Secret Service says he awoke about 6:30 a.m., had lunch at his Washington home, and spent the day there...."

They all agree and press reports confirm that Bush delivered his speech at the Capitol Hilton in Washington. The vice-presidential candidate was present. Secret Service records show Bush arrived at either 7 or at 8:12 p.m.

Monday, October 20, 1980: Bush arrived that morning at Tweed-New Haven Airport for two days of campaigning in Connecticut. He met with factory workers at Avco Lycoming in Stratford before moving to Sacred Heart University in Bridgeport. There, he told students, "Frankly, [the Reagan campaign has] been concerned about [the possibility of an October Surprise].... But as the election draws closer and closer, we don't know what [Carter's] going to do."

While it might seem unlikely that Bush would take an overnight trip to Paris in the last two weeks of a presidential campaign to make a treasonous arms-for-hostages deal with revolutionary Iranians, the risks to Bush, and Reagan, if discovered, would have been disastrous, but it certainly *was* technically possible. Bush could have left either from Andrews Air Force Base or Washington National Airport Saturday night and completed the seven-hour flight, given the six-hour time difference, by 11 a.m. Sunday. To be back in Washington, D.C., by 6 p.m. local time (allowing for an 8 1/2-hour flight and one hour to get ready for his 7 p.m. dinner), Bush could have left France as late as 3:30 p.m. Paris time giving him a tight four and a half hours in which to meet at the Hotel Florida.

If true, the October Surprise could be a major scandal. Deliberate actions by private citizens to prevent the release of American hostages could lead to charges of treason and kidnapping. There is also evidence that Reagan-Bush campaign officials were informed illegally by insiders in the National Security Council and Senate Intelligence Committee about the hostage negotiations. Former President Carter told Robert Morris of the *Village Voice* that he believes Donald Gregg, then a national security aide and later national security adviser to Vice President Bush, was one of the officials who kept the Reagan-Bush campaign informed about the Administration's moves to free the hostages.

Carter believes that Gregg and a number of former CIA officials may have organized a vendetta against his Administration, which had fired hundreds of CIA agents in an attempt to reform the agency. "We tried to clean up the CIA," the former President told the *Voice*. "It had been shot through with people that were later involved with the Iran-contra affair; people like Secord and so forth...." The cashiered CIA agents were loyal to former CIA Director Bush, Carter said.[3]

---

3   Robert Morris, "Behind the October Surprise," *Village Voice*, May 21, 1991, p. 31.

Despite persistent allegations reported by *In These Times, Z Magazine* and other periodicals, the mass media ignored the story until April, when an op-ed article by former national security aide Gary Sick in the New York Times and a PBS *Frontline* documentary by investigative journalist Robert Parry gave the allegations new credibility.

Sick, a Navy officer attached to the Carter Administration's National Security Council as a Middle East expert, is now an adjunct professor of Middle East politics at Columbia University. Sick says he dismissed the allegations at first, but thought the timing of the hostage release 30 minutes after Reagan took office "was peculiar."

"We had reports later on that the people holding the hostages in fact were standing with watches, waiting at the airport, to make sure that the time had passed, that Carter was no longer President, before releasing the hostages," he told *Frontline*.

Years later, Sick's research for a book on the hostage crisis convinced him that the early reports of a deal between the Reagan campaign and the Iranians were accurate. Sick says that he has interviewed about 15 separate sources who claim to know of the secret negotiations between the Reagan-Bush campaign and the Iranians. A number of the sources are "respectable people," Sick told *Frontline*.

Other sources were "money movers, arms dealers, low-level intelligence operatives, people who work undercover and who, for one reason or another, are now dissatisfied with their lot and are prepared to talk about some of what they knew, perhaps with considerable exaggeration. Finally," Sick said, "I...passed a point where it was harder to explain away the people who were supposedly all lying to me for reasons that I couldn't understand than it was to believe that something in fact happened."

The hostages were seized in 1979 by Iranian radicals who wanted to disrupt relations between Iran's revolutionary government, then still in the hands of moderate reformers, and the United States. At first, the nation rallied around Carter's economic and diplomatic measures to pressure Iran to free the Americans, but in April, 1980, a secret military rescue mission failed.

The hostage-taking was exploited by the Reagan-Bush campaign as an example of national humiliation and weakness. But Reagan campaign officials told *Frontline* they were afraid the Carter Administration would engineer the release of the hostages before the election — an "October Surprise," in the words of Bush, to deprive the Republicans of their best campaign issues.

Sick's allegations center on William Casey, chairman of the Reagan campaign and for six years Director of Central Intelligence in the Reagan-Bush Administration. Casey, who died in 1987, reportedly met with Iranian representatives in Madrid and Paris before the November election.

One important source for this is Jamshid Hashemi, an Iranian arms dealer. Hashemi says he and his brother Cyrus organized two meetings in July 1980 between Casey and an important Iranian cleric, Mehdi Karrubi. Karrubi is now speaker of the Iranian parliament. The meetings were held in a Madrid hotel room.

Hashemi says Casey's proposal was "blunt." "Casey said the Iranians should hold the hostages until after the election and the Reagan Administration would behave favorably towards Iran, releasing military equipment and the frozen Iranian assets," he told *Frontline*. Karrubi and Casey returned to Madrid in August when the Iranian cleric "expressed acceptance," Hashemi said. "The hostages would be released after Carter's defeat." Hashemi's account of the meetings has been confirmed by two other sources, Sick wrote in the *Times*.

At about the same time as the Casey-Karrubi meetings in Madrid, Sick wrote, "individuals associated with the Reagan campaign made contact with senior government officials in Israel, which agreed to act as the channel for the arms deliveries to Iran that Casey had promised." Sick cited two former Israeli intelligence officers as his sources.

Is Hashemi lying about the Casey meetings? If he is, not even the severest critics of the "October Surprise" allegations have been able to explain why the Iranian arms dealer would deliberately mislead Sick. Hashemi is not under indictment or facing any charges.

Hashemi is not the only source of the meetings between Casey and Iranian representatives. *Frontline* interviewed Arif Durrani, an arms dealer now serving a 10-year sentence in Federal prison for selling arms to Iran. According to Durrani, Iranian officials told him Karrubi met in Spain with Casey. Another source, retired Israeli intelligence officer Ari Ben-Menashe, claims to have seen intelligence reports on Casey's trip to Madrid. "The Americans agreed to release money and make promises for the future when Reagan-Bush take over [sic] to make relations better," he told *Frontline*, "and the Americans also promised that they will allow arms shipments to Iran.... And this is why Israel was brought in."

Even though the fundamentalist Iranian Government was a sworn enemy of the Jewish state, Israel feared Iraq's growing military power in the region. In the mid-1980s Israel was the source of weapons shipped to Iran during the Iran-Contra affair.

Retired Air Force Gen. Richard Secord secretly channeled the profits from these sales to finance the contra war against Nicaragua. But if the "October Surprise" allegations are true, Israel actually began in late 1980 or early 1981 to supply the Iranians with arms as part of the deal negotiated between Iran and the Reagan-Bush campaign.

In mid-September 1980 Iraq invaded Iran. The Iranians, now desperate for military supplies, sent an emissary to Washington. Sick's sources speculate the Iranians were following two tracks, negotiating simultaneously with the U.S. Government and the Reagan-Bush campaign.

Sadegh Tabatabai, Khomeini's emissary to the United States, told *Frontline* that he and the State department quickly reached agreement on a *quid pro quo*: the hostages would be returned and the United States would release Iranian assets and arms deliveries frozen by the Carter Administration. "At the end of the talks, I was very optimistic," Tabatabai said. "Carter had accepted the conditions set by the Iranians." The atmosphere seemed favorable for the agreement. The United States wanted the hostages, and Iran needed military supplies.

This arrangement resembled the deal Casey allegedly proposed in Madrid, but there was one important difference. The Administration's formula involved the immediate liberation of the hostages, while Reagan wanted to stall the release until *after* the election. Former Iranian President Abolhassan Bani-Sadr told *Frontline* that "[i]f there had not been contacts with the Reagan-Bush group, the hostages would have been freed six months before the U.S. elections."

Despite agreement between Washington and Teheran on the hostage arms *quid pro quo*, the Iranian government put the issue on ice.

Final agreement reached

What happened? In October, according to Sick's reconstruction, Casey met in Paris with representatives of the Iranian and Israeli governments. An agreement was reached on the proposals advanced earlier in Madrid. Iran would not release the hostages until after the election, and Israel would ship arms and spare parts to Iran.

For years Richard Brenneke said the Agency ordered him to Paris in October, 1980, to launder money for the Reagan-Bush deal with the Iranians. The CIA denies the Agency ever employed Brenneke.

In a September 10 *Village Voice* story banner-headlined **BRENNEKE EXPOSED**, Frank Snepp damaged Brenneke's credibility. He discovered while examining credit card and other receipts, that Brenneke was *apparently* charging meals and motel rooms in Portland and Seattle during many of the times he claimed he was in Paris and elsewhere during 1980.

Even though the receipts indicated he was not where he claimed to have been, Brenneke's information was accurate. *October Surprise* author Barbara Honegger, who is familiar with the story, questions how thoroughly Snepp verified that the receipts were signed by Brenneke, and claims Snepp admitted he had made no effort to verify Brenneke's whereabouts during that period.

Snepp and his editor at the *Village Voice*, Dan Bischoff, were unwilling to provide receipts to Barbara Honegger for verification of Brenneke's signature and purported activities, claiming they were holding them for a television special. Honegger also claims Snepp advised her following her press conference in Washington, D.C., in August 1988 to drop her investigation because her activities were "threatening an important covert operation."

Brenneke told *Frontline*, that while in Paris, Casey approved the Iranian Government's shopping list and explained how private funds could buy weapons for Iran: "There was, and I added this up as I went along, somewhere between $35 million and $40 million that was going to change hands. That is, it would wind up being used for the purchase of weapons to be...delivered to Iran.... Casey at the time told me that I would have the authority to withdraw funds from a Mexican bank and he says 'There probably will be an American bank or two involved in this whole thing.' He said 'yes' on virtually every hand-held weapon that was asked for. He limited the number of TOW missiles in the initial shipments.... Tires were a big item."

Did Bush accompany his future national security adviser to Paris? "At least five of the sources who say they were in Paris for these meetings insist that Bush was present for at least one," Sick wrote in the *Times*. "Three of the sources say they saw him there."

Brenneke says he did not see Bush in Paris but was told by Heinrich Rupp that he was there. Ari Ben-Menashe, the former Israeli intelligence officer, also claims he saw Bush in Paris that weekend.

If Bush did not travel to Paris it should be a simple matter for the White House to prove where he was on that weekend. Bush, then a candidate for Vice President, was under 24-hour Secret Service guard. Records should be available to document every day of the campaign. Bush described the allegations as "grossly untrue, actually incorrect, bald-faced lies" and insists he can "categorically deny any contact with the Iranians or anything having to do with it." But, astonishingly, the White House has circulated a number of contradictory alibis for the dates Bush allegedly met with the Iranians.

During the Brenneke trial, for example, two Secret Service witnesses testified that they were protecting Bush in the United States when the Paris meetings reportedly took place. Under cross examination, the agents said they could not recall seeing Bush that weekend, and they also could not recall whether they were even on duty. The Government also failed to produce any records proving the agents were with Bush or that Bush was in the country.

Other conflicting accounts have surfaced:

- *Frontline* obtained "heavily censored Secret Service documents" that showed Bush's Secret Service detail spent the weekend at a suburban country club outside Washington, D.C. The records do not specify who was in the party and do not mention Bush.
- The *Washington Times* reported that "Reagan-Bush campaign records, independently confirmed" by the newspaper, proved that Bush spent Sunday, Oct. 19, at home. "The Secret Service says he awoke about 6:30 a.m., had lunch at his Washington home and spent the day there preparing [a] speech. He returned home from the speech about 9 p.m." the *Times* reported.
- Also on May 8 columnist L. Gordon Crovitz, a member of the *Wall Street Journal* editorial board, wrote that on Oct. 19 Bush had lunch at the Supreme Court with Justice Potter Stewart and his wife. Stewart is now dead, his wife

reportedly suffers from chronic memory loss and no office records or diaries exist to support this alibi. Christic Institute, *Convergence*, Summer 1991.

In the fall of 1990 in Manhattan's Southern District Court, another chapter in the Iran-Contra drama quietly played out. Ari Ben-Menashe had been charged by the U.S. government with attempting to sell in April 1989 three military transport airplanes belonging to Israel, to a man who claimed to represent Iran, but was actually a U.S. Customs agent. Ben-Menashe claimed in court that he was an Israeli agent working for Israeli Prime Minister Yitzhak Shamir.

A former *Time* reporter named Rajiz Samghabadi proved to be the most compelling witness for the 39-year-old Ben-Menashe, testifying that Ben-Menashe had told him in early 1986 about the Reagan administration's arms deals with Iran to free the hostages. On Nov. 3, 1986, the Lebanese newspaper *Al Shiraa* printed an account confirming those arms deals.

Samghabadi further stated to the Manhattan court: "Ben-Menashe consistently tried to get a story in print [in *Time* magazine] saying that as of 1980 there was a huge conspiracy between the U.S. government and Israel to supply Iran with billions of dollars of weapons off the books, without legal channels knowing anything about them and it was still continuing at the time he talked to me.... He was extremely perturbed that despite highly specific information, *Time* editors refused to run that story."

That story was about the alleged deal between the 1980 Reagan-Bush campaign and Khomeini to delay the release of the hostages. Joel Bleifuss interviewed Samghabadi several times in 1988, during which he professed knowledge of such a deal but would provide no particulars.[4]

Ben-Menashe was found not guilty after a six-week trial that garnered little media attention. Nonetheless, he had been pun-

---

4   Joel Bleifuss, *In These Times*, October 12, 1988.

ished, spending eleven months and three weeks in jail awaiting trial. According to federal sentencing guidelines, the arms-dealing crime for which he was charged carried a recommended 15-month sentence.

Bleifuss interviewed Ben-Menashe at his home in Lexington, Ky. The Israeli operative had decided to publicize his carefully-guarded secrets after 14 years, he explained, because "I was left to hang dry here in the States. So many people have died. So many people have gone to jail. Cover-up after Cover-up, it keeps going on and on. The time has come to stop this."[5]

In early 1980, acknowledged Ben-Menashe, both the Carter administration and the Republicans who hoped to capture the White House wanted to make a deal with the Iranians to release the hostages. To reach an agreement with Iran, the Carter administration asked Iranian arms dealer Cyrus Hashemi and his two brothers to serve as intermediaries.

"But Carter and his boys were doing all the wrong things," says Ben-Menashe. "The Hashemi brothers were basically frauds. They had enough connections to sell arms to the Iranians, but they didn't have the connections to get the hostages out. They needed real connections to Khomeini and the approval of different factions in the Supreme Council."

Working for the Republicans, says Ben Menashe, were Carter intelligence officers who had worked with Bush when he was CIA director from 1976 to 1977.

According to Ben-Menashe, Carter made a mistake when he named Stansfield Turner to replace Bush as CIA director. Carter should have made "sure that all the Bush people were thrown out." Carter had earned the enmity of many CIA officers following his house cleaning of the agency prompted by congressional investigations into earlier CIA misdeeds.

Two of the CIA officers Ben-Menashe says Carter should

---

5   Joel Bleifuss, "Truth: The Last Hostage," *In These Times*, April 17-23, 1991.

have dumped were Donald Gregg and Robert Gates, both of whom held prominent positions under Carter and later Reagan. Gregg, a career CIA officer, served as the CIA's chief of station in Korea during Bush's tenure at the CIA. At the time of the hostage crisis, Gregg worked in Carter's National Security Council as CIA liaison. After the election, he was named Vice President Bush's national security adviser. He now serves as ambassador to Korea.

Gates, also a career CIA officer, served on Ford's NSC. Under Carter he remained at the NSC and was later executive assistant to CIA Director Turner. Gates' career prospered under Reagan's CIA director and 1980 campaign manager, William Casey. Gates now is Bush's CIA director after having served as deputy national security adviser.

"In early 1980, it was already clear that it was going to be a Reagan-Bush ticket," says Ben-Menashe, who explains that this information was contained in an intelligence-community circular and attributed to Ezra Weitzman, Prime Minister Begin's defense minister. Weitzman said that Bush had confided this to some friends in Israel.

According to Ben-Menashe, in early 1980 two Republican campaign representatives approached Iran about striking a deal. One was Robert McFarlane. Ben-Menashe, in a deposition for a federal case in 1991, stated that McFarlane had a special [paid] relationship with Israel since 1978, when he worked as an aide for the late Sen. John Tower (R-TX). Subsequently, McFarlane told Phil Linsalata of the *St. Louis Post-Dispatch* that Ben-Menashe's accusation is "absolutely false." However, *In These Times* reported the FBI was investigating the allegation that McFarlane was an Israeli agent.

According to Ben-Menashe, the other Republican representative was Dr. Earl Brian, a former Secretary of Health and Welfare for California under Gov. Reagan who left public service in 1974 allegedly to deal arms to the Shah's Iran. Brian, says Ben-Menashe, was connected to Iranian Prime Minister

Mehdi Bazaragan, who resigned after the American hostages were taken in Teheran but continued to play a prominent role in Iran's government. Both men, says Ben-Menashe, "worked very closely" with Gates, then an aide to CIA Director Turner.

In February 1980, says Ben-Menashe, McFarlane and Brian traveled to Teheran to arrange meetings between Casey and representatives of Khomeini. According to Ben-Menashe, between March and September 1980, Casey met with Iran's Ayatollah Mehdi Karrubi four times in Spain to discuss the following deal: Iran would hold the hostages until after the election, and in return, the Reagan administration, after taking office, would release frozen Iranian assets and provide Iran with U.S. weapons.

It was not, however, decided how the weapons would be transferred to Iran via a third party. Karrubi is now speaker of the Iranian parliament. *Frontline*, using other sources, reports that Casey and Karrubi met twice in Madrid, once in July and once in August 1980.

That August, the Iranians struck a similar but separate deal with the Carter administration. CIA Director Turner told *Frontline* that the Carter administration negotiated with Sadegh Tabatabai, a young businessman related to the Ayatollah Khomeini through marriage. Tabatabai told *Frontline*, "At the end of the talks, I was very optimistic Carter had accepted the conditions set by the Iranians."

Parry reports on *Frontline*, "The Iranian offer mirrored the agreement that Casey had allegedly accepted in Madrid." But after striking the Carter deal, the Iranians expressed little interest in finishing it before the 1980 election.

Although Begin had respected Carter's wishes since April 1980 and curtailed arms deals with Iran, Israel's prime minister changed his mind that August, throwing his support to the Republicans.

According to Ben-Menashe, Begin wrote a directive that Israel would help gain the release of the hostages by supporting "the efforts made by various Americans who are not necessarily members of the present administration." Ben-Menashe says he saw that directive, which was distributed on a "need-to-know basis." He also says Begin's decision was made very hesitantly. Ben-Menashe claims that the Israelis realized their involvement could be interpreted as subverting "legal government in the U.S."

Ben-Menashe says that CIA Director Turner asked Begin to aid the Republican negotiating team. Turner, says Ben-Menashe, led Begin to believe that he would continue to head the CIA under a Reagan-Bush administration. Turner has denied this. On Oct. 2, 1980, Ben-Menashe says he met three members of the Reagan-Bush campaign at the L'Enfant Plaza Hotel in Washington, D.C. He says he presented the three — McFarlane, Richard Allen and Lawrence Silberman — with an alternative to the deal Casey had negotiated in Madrid. Ben-Menashe says that the Israelis had arranged this deal with Iran because they had qualms about helping the Republicans subvert the Carter administration's negotiations with the Iranians for the hostages' release.

At the time, McFarlane was working for Sen. Tower on the Senate Armed Services Committee. McFarlane later served as Reagan's national security adviser. McFarlane negotiated the 1985 secret arms-for-hostages negotiations with Iran. In 1980, Allen was the Reagan-Bush campaign's foreign-policy adviser. Silberman, an Allen aide during the 1980 campaign, was later appointed to the federal judiciary.

A photocopy of Ben-Menashe's notes on the meeting reads, in part, "Oct. 2, 1980. Eastern Shuttle, D.C. E. Plaza Hotel.... To meet Silberman, Allen, Bob McFar. 40 page document F-14 parts already paid for, in return of the hostages. Swap in Karachi. Charter 707." According to Ben-Menashe, the Iranians had told the Israelis that they would release the hostages immediately in exchange for U.S.-made F-14 parts that Iran, under the shah, had already paid for.

He says that the three Americans "turned that deal down" because the Americans "wanted the hostages held until after the election. The Iranians were dying to get rid of the hostages. But the Americans wanted to strike their own deal, not an Israeli one, with the Iranians, so they threw that one out and struck their own deal later [that month] in Paris."

Over the past four years, Allen, McFarlane and Silberman have acknowledged that they met an Iranian representative at L'Enfant Plaza Hotel in early October, 1980, and were told that his country was willing to release the hostages to the Reagan campaign. All three have insisted that they dismissed the offer and they don't remember the name of the man. Allen says he lost his minutes of the meeting. He told *Frontline*, "Eventually I'll be able to find the memorandum I wrote on this meeting, but I haven't been able to find it yet."

Ben-Menashe said he was accompanied at this meeting by the late Houshang Lavi, an Iranian-born arms dealer who had previously brokered multibillion-dollar U.S weapons sales to Iran. But Ben-Menashe says Lavi, an Israeli agent, did not participate. Lavi, however, told *Frontline* he met with the three Americans.

The alleged deal that Casey had pursued during his meetings in Spain with the Ayatollah's representative Karrubi was completed at a gathering of Americans, Israelis and Iranians in Paris on Oct. 18-22, 1980, says Ben-Menashe. He says he was a member of the Israeli group. The Israelis, five men and one woman, attended at Casey's request. He needed them to coordinate the arms deliveries to Iran. According to Ben-Menashe, "My job was basically to put together an address book of all the Iranians at the meetings."

Ben-Menashe told *Frontline*, "The Iranians were basically willing to release the hostages immediately. The Americans were saying, 'We cannot release the money so quickly.... Keep the hostages until January. It will take time to release the money. Let's set a date in January for the release.' The Iranians were saying, 'Just give us the money and you can get your guys.'" Ben-Menashe refuses to name all the people at the meetings but says the delegation included Casey and Bush.

Richard Brenneke also claims to have been at one of those meetings. In a deposition for a 1988 federal court case in Denver, he said, "The purpose of that meeting was to negotiate not only for the release of the hostages but also to discuss...how we would go about satisfying everybody involved."

According to Brenneke, the Americans at the session included Casey and Gregg. Gregg became Bush's national security adviser. Brenneke also said that he heard from his friend, Heinrich Rupp, an American pilot who claims he flew Casey to Paris, that Bush was in France at the time. At Brenneke's perjury trial, the U.S. attorney failed to prove that Gregg, Casey and Bush were in Paris on Oct. 18-22, 1980. The Justice Department was also unable to provide Casey with an alibi. Gregg's claim fell apart also, following the meteorologist's testimony.

The testimony of the two Secret Service agents was not convincing. Brenneke's lawyer, Michael Scott, told *Frontline*, "They had two Secret Service witnesses testify that they were on the Secret Service team that was protecting the vice-presidential candidate, George Bush, at the time. They didn't remember what hours they worked. They thought they were on duty that weekend, but they couldn't be sure.... They weren't sure that they saw George Bush at any time during that weekend."

Parry reported for *Frontline* that he obtained "heavily censored Secret Service documents...that show that Bush's detail went to a suburban country club [that weekend]. But the papers do not specify with whom the candidate might have met, nor do they supply any other details as to who was actually in the party."

Gary Sick, Carter's NSC point man on the Teheran hostage crisis in his version of the 1980 hostage negotiations in *October Surprise*, told *Frontline*, "I think it was something like 15 people that claim personal knowledge that this [the deal] happened.... There are a very large number of very respectable people who really do believe that this happened.. I finally, I guess, passed a point where it was harder to explain away the people who were supposedly all lying to me for reasons that I couldn't understand than it was to believe that something in fact happened."

Sick experienced fallout from the alleged deal. Carter aides negotiating details of the concurrent Carter deal in October 1980 noted a shift in the Iranian bargaining position. In 1988 Sick told reporters that by Oct. 22, 1980 the Iranians had changed their demands from spare parts for military equipment to cash. Such a shift would make sense if Iran knew it would have access to U.S.-made arms during the Reagan administration.

On Nov. 28, 1980, Ben-Menashe says he was appointed to the IDFMI-Mossad Joint Committee for Iran-Israel Relations. He joined five others on the committee, four of whom he says he had worked with in Paris the previous month. He says, "Between that date and September 1987, I was executing an official policy of the Israeli government, in other words, gun-running."

Arms sales to Iran via Israel began soon after Reagan took office, according to Ben-Menashe.

Nicholas Veliotis was assistant secretary of state for the Middle East at the beginning of the Reagan administration. He told *Frontline*, "My own firsthand knowledge starts when I'm assistant secretary of state in early February 1981.... Within a few months, we received a press report from TASS that an Argentinean plane had crashed and, according to the document, crashed in Soviet territory. This was chartered by Israel, and it was carrying American military equipment to Iran."

On July 23, 1981, the *Jerusalem Post* reported that an Argentinean cargo plane was shot down over Soviet airspace as it returned to Tel Aviv from Teheran. Subsequently it was reported that the plane had been transporting $30 million worth of U.S.-made M-48 tank parts and ammunition to Iran.[6]

October Surprise, Barbara Honegger's watershed exposé; Gary Sick's book by the same title; *Witness*, by Mansur Rhafizadeh, former head of the Iranian SAVAK in the U.S.; the

---

6   Bleifuss, "Arms business as usual: guns to Iran since 1980," *In These Times*, October 12, 1988.

new book by former Iranian President Abolhassan Bani-Sadr; and the October 1988 *Playboy* article, *"An Election Held Hostage,"* by Abbie Hoffman and Jonathan Silvers, that may have cost Hoffman his life; all recount in detail the events that led to the delay of the hostages' release and the flow of ultimately billions of dollars worth of U.S. weapons to Iran.

According to Hoffman and Silvers:

> As early as February 1981, Secretary of State Alexander Haig was briefed on Israeli arms sales to Iran. In November, Defense Minister Ariel Sharon asked Haig to approve the sale of F-14 parts to Teheran. While the proposal was in direct opposition to publicized Administration objectives, Sharon pitched it as a way of gaining favor with Iranian "moderates." According to *The Washington Post*, Haig was ambivalent, but consented with the approval of top officials, notably Robert McFarlane.
>
> Israeli Ambassador Moshe Arens later told *The Boston Globe* that Iranian arms sales had been approved at "almost the highest levels" of U.S. Government in spring 1981. In fact, Reagan's Senior Interdepartmental Group agreed in July 1981 that the U.S. should encourage third-party arms sales to Iran to "advance U.S. interests in the Middle East." The initiative was such a reversal of policy that it's unlikely Haig would have consented without the President's approval. Haig refuses to comment.
>
> In November 1986, the Administration finally said the Israelis had delivered U.S. military supplies to Iran in the early Eighties. The State Department downplayed the sales, claiming that the amount of arms Iran received was trivial, that only $10 million or $15 million worth of non-lethal aid had reached Iran. That figure was disputed. The *New York Times* estimated that before 1983, Iran received $2.8 billion in supplies from nine countries, including the U.S. A West German newspaper placed the figure closer to $500 million. Bani-Sadr said that his administration alone received $50 million worth of parts. Houshang Lavi [an Iranian arms dealer recently deceased] believes Khomeini got at least $500 million in military supplies.

Lavi is [was] in a position to know. In 1981, he and Israeli arms dealer Yacobi Nimrodi reportedly sold HAWK missiles and guidance systems to Iran. In April and October 1981, Western Dynamics International, a Long Island company run by Lavi's brother, contracted to sell the Iranian Air Force $16 million worth of bomb fuses and F-14 parts. Admiral Bobby Ray Inman, William Casey's Deputy Director of Central Intelligence, said that the CIA knew in 1981 that Israel and private arms dealers were making sizable deliveries to Iran. The Reagan White House raised no objections.

Eighteen months after Reagan took office, Iran had received virtually all the spare parts and weapons that Carter had refused to include in his hostage accord.

It is not known who authorized the sales to Iran. Nicholas Veliotis told *Frontline*, "It was clear to me after my conversations with people on high that indeed we had agreed that the Israelis could trans-ship to Iran some American-origin military equipment."

Haig put it this way to *Frontline*, "I have the sneaking suspicion that somebody in the White House winked."

In 1984, a coalition government in Israel between the Likud and Labor parties was formed, and Labor leader Shimon Peres began serving a two-year term as prime minister. "At the time Peres tried to wrest the ongoing U.S. arms sales to Iran out of the hands of the middlemen in the Israeli intelligence community. That way, he could turn the sales over to his own cronies, who were half-private contractors," says Ben-Menashe, who adds that Israeli arms merchants Adolph Schwimmer and Yacobi Nimrodi were two of Peres' cronies.

According to Ben-Menashe, Peres' move created an arms channel that tried to compete with the one operated by the Joint Committee, for which Ben-Menashe worked. The channel operated out of the office of Amiram Nir, who served as Peres' anti-terrorism adviser. Nimrodi and Schwimmer worked with Nir to set up the channel.

In spring 1985, Michael Ledeen, a part-time consultant to

Reagan's NSC, and McFarlane, Reagan's then-NSC adviser and a man whom Ben-Menashe alleges had a "special relationship" with Israel that dates from 1977, introduced Oliver North, Reagan's NSC operative, to Nir, Nimrodi and Schwimmer. They helped North and others in the White House set up the 1985 and 1986 arms-for-hostages deals to free the Americans held in Lebanon.

These two competing arms channels posed a problem for Bush and his former CIA colleagues who, says Ben-Menashe, had been "controlling and sitting on the Joint Committee's operation since Bush became vice president." However, Ben-Menashe says, Bush did not want to defy Israel's reigning prime minister, so he didn't interfere with the Nir-North deals.

But Nir and North's arms deals were not as lucrative as the Joint Committee's, says Ben-Menashe. "They connected with the wrong Iranians." According to Ben-Menashe, the Joint Committee sold 12,000 TOW missiles to Iran in three batches over four years while during the same period Nir and North managed to provide Iran with only 100 TOWs and some HAWK surface-to-air missiles, which were returned by the Iranians to Israel because they were not acceptable since they were decorated with Stars of David.

To consolidate the arms business and wipe out the competition, North, in 1986, ordered a U.S. Customs Service sting operation. The sting put arms dealers who worked with Israel's Joint Committee temporarily out of business.

The sting was approved by Rudolph Giuliani, the U.S. Attorney for the Southern District of New York. The point man was Cyrus Hashemi, who had been indicted in 1984 by a federal grand jury for allegedly violating the Arms Export Control Act. In November 1985, Hashemi had approached Giuliani with this deal: he would go undercover for the Customs Service if Giuliani would drop the year-old charges against him.

Michael Finnegan, a New York-based researcher, reports that an attorney employed by the U.S. Senate who requested anonymity said that North and others in the NSC were aware of the "sting" and had a "vested interest" in Customs using Hashemi to "shut down elements of competition."

On April 21, 1986, the sting went down. That day the U.S. Customs Service arrested 17 Israeli, European and American arms dealers lured to Bermuda by Hashemi. Giuliani later indicted 13 of the dealers for conspiring to sell Iran $2 billion in missiles, fighter aircraft, tanks, guns and spare parts.

Included in the 13 were four men Ben-Menashe says were connected to Israel's Joint Committe: Brig. Gen. Abraham Bar'am; Samuel Evans, the lawyer for Saudi arms dealer Adnan Khashoggi; and two Israelis, Rafael Eisenberg and his son Guriel. Ben-Menashe says he had also planned to travel to the Bermuda meeting, but was warned to stay away by John DeLaroque, an arms dealer indicted in the sting but not apprehended in Bermuda.

Ben-Menashe says he and other Israeli intelligence officers convinced Giuliani to release the indicted Israelis from New York's Metropolitan Correctional Center where they were being held. They vowed to get even with North for allowing the sting to proceed.

To achieve these ends, Ben-Menashe says that he leaked the story of the White House's 1985 and 1986 arms-for-hostages deals.

On Nov. 3, 1986, the Beirut newspaper *Al Shiraa* published an article detailing the secret deals with Iran. Journalist Richard Ryan, using sources other than Ben-Menashe, reported how the Israelis got even with North in "Revenge is Revenge; the exclusive story of how the Israelis leaked Irangate to save their agents."[7]

After the *Al Shiraa* story exposed the Iran-contra deals, the arms dealers were released on bail. The charges were dropped in 1989.

Despite their long standing differences on the Palestinian

---

7   *In These Times,* February 11, 1987.

issue, Israel's Labor and Likud parties agreed on one thing: military support for Iran was crucial to Israel's stability. "Iran was our main card in the Middle east. It was a deadly enemy for the Arabs. They were the ones who could hold the Arabs at bay," says Ben-Menashe.

But Israel's support for Iran was not shared by everyone in the White House. "The Bush people had it in for Israel, or rather, the Likud, since Likud was running the show," says Ben-Menashe. He believes that one goal of Bush and his former CIA colleagues was to maintain friendly relations with the Arabs and their oil. To further that goal, the Bush group established Iraq as a dominant power in the Middle east, according to Ben-Menashe.

The U.S. attitude toward Iraq began to warm in 1982, when the Reagan Administration removed the country from its list of terrorist nations. In late 1983, high-level American officials began to travel to Baghdad, and in 1984, the U.S. started supporting the Iraqi war effort against Iran by supplying intelligence to Iraq.

In May 1984, Saddam Hussein stated that Iraq was using intelligence provided by AWACS flown by American pilots based in Saudi Arabia. In November 1984, the U.S. restored diplomatic relations with Iraq. Around this time Saddam Hussein announced that he was willing to join the Camp David peace process.

Administration policy makers believed a powerful Iraq could accomplish two U.S. goals: Act as a regional balance to Israel, and pressure Israel to reach an accommodation with the Palestinians.

Throughout their partnership in the 1984 coalition government, the Likud and Labor parties were split on the Palestinian issue. Labor was willing to negotiate an international conference on the Palestinian issue and leaned toward a Palestinian state on the West Bank. Likud supported a Palestinian state in what is now Jordan.

According to Ben-Menashe, the U.S. attempted to empower

Iraq by allegedly supplying it, through third parties such as Chile, with chemicals it needed for chemical weapons. "The Americans are giving chemicals to Iraq to maintain a balance of terror and convince Israel that it couldn't last with just military might. This could force the Israelis into a peace plan. That was the deal," he says. "Even today the Bush administration is keeping Hussein intact in order that he remains a perceived threat to Israel."

William Northrop, a self-described colonel in Israeli military intelligence, says President Carter, approved an Israeli military shipment to Iran in the hostage crisis in mid-1980. The arms expert who played a role in the Iran-contra affair told a federal court that the Carter administration backed an Israeli arms shipment to Iran *before* the 1980 election at the time the Republicans were purportedly bargaining to forestall an early release of the 52 American hostages in Teheran.

Northrop also stated, in an affidavit obtained by the *Village Voice*, that within weeks of the inauguration and the freeing of the hostages, the Reagan White House okayed huge Israeli arms shipments to the ayatollah, though such deliveries were banned on November 13, 1979. The allegation, denied by former Carter officials, raises the prospect that the Carter White House inadvertently gave the Israelis a green light to tamper with the negotiations to free the 52 American hostages.

The picture Northrop draws is of massive U.S.-Israeli collusion in breaching the U.S. arms embargo against Iran long before Lt. Col. Oliver North became involved in late 1985. Since congressional Iran-contra investigators never looked into the early deals, Northrop's testimony provides a piece of the puzzle barely glimpsed.

It also complicates debate over the "October Surprise" charges. Northrop's account does not contradict these allegations. But in raising the possibility that the Carter administration also approved Israeli shipments to Iran, he casts the Israelis, not the Republicans, as spoilers. Indeed, if his testimony proves accurate, it would appear that both sides in the 1980 presidential race allowed the Israelis a free hand in pursuing covert arms policies that affected U.S. politics.

In a recent phone conversation, Sick elaborated, saying that Carter sent a message to Begin on October 23, 1980 protesting the Israeli shipment of aircraft tires, and was advised the following day that the cargo had already departed for Iran. "Technically speaking," said Sick, "Carter approved the transaction in the sense that he didn't break off relations with Israel." But, Sick emphasized, there had been no explicit approval. That being said, however, he refused to discount Northrop's allegations. Indeed, he argued that the Israelis may have been misled about Carter's position on arms shipments by rogue CIA agents acting behind the President's back. These agents, he speculated, may have duped the Israelis into believing they could resupply Iran with Carter's blessing in order to derail the President's last-minute hostage negotiations.

Northrop does not mention in his affidavit any of the alleged Republican "October Surprise" efforts to delay a hostage release. But he does say that in December 1980, before the Reagan inauguration, Israel's military attache in Washington, Menachem Meron, sounded out the incoming administration on its policy toward Iranian arms sales. Northrop says the query was passed on to Reagan aide Richard Allen through a member of the American Israel Political Action Committee, Morris Amitay.

Like several other events mentioned in Northrop's affidavit, the Allen-Amitay exchange has been previously reported. But in contrast to other published accounts of the conversation, Northrop insists that the Reagan official gave a thumbs-up to the deliveries. "Allen checked [with his superiors]," says Northrop "and advised Amitay of the new administration's approval."

Ultimately, the Justice Department dropped its case against him and other defendants in early 1989, after congressional Iran-contra revelations indicated that the Reagan administration had engaged in arms-for-hostage deals with Iran.

In the summer of 1992, Congressional investigators concluded that "all credible evidence" contradicts claims that President Bush went to Paris personally in 1980 to delay the release of American hostages. Their findings came despite the testimony of several people, including an Israeli arms dealer and a man claiming to have flown on secret government missions, who said they saw Bush in Paris on Oct. 19 or 20, 1980.

Despite these findings, the House task force said it would continue its investigation on whether the Reagan-Bush campaign conspired with Iran to delay the release of the 52 American captives to deny President Carter a potential boost toward re-election. The head of the Task Force, Rep. Lee Hamilton, said interest in allegations about Bush was so high that the group decided to publicly release their conclusions.

CHAPTER 6

"Just Fly Low"

"Well, George, I go in looking for prisoners, but I spend all my time discovering the government has been moving drugs around the world and is involved in illegal arms deals...I can't get at the prisoners because of the corruption among our own covert people."

Texas billionaire H. Ross Perot to then-Vice President George Bush in 1987, when Bush asked Perot how his investigation into missing Vietnam POWs was going

"For 7½ years I've worked alongside Reagan, and I'm proud to be his partner. We've had triumphs, we've made mistakes, we've ahs SEX...uh, I mean SETBACKS, we've had setbacks."

Vice President George Bush, May 6, 1987

"I fear I owe you an apology," C.L. Sulzberger of the *New York Times* wrote to poet Allen Ginsberg on April 11, 1978. "I have been reading a succession of pieces about CIA involvement in the dope trade in Southeast Asia and I remember when you first suggested I look into this I thought you were full of beans. Indeed you were right."

The nation's newspaper of record may have forgotten what its foreign affairs columnist learned. The *Times* reported only recently that the CIA had been dragooned into George Bush's drug wars after years on the sidelines. The agency's chief spokesperson, James Greenleaf, said that for the CIA, "narcotics is a

95

new priority."

That's not quite accurate. The CIA *has* long been involved in the drug wars. It's just been mostly on the other side.

Drugs are an old priority of the agency, dating back to when the wartime Office of Strategic Services (OSS), the CIA's father figure, and its sister agency, the Office of Naval Intelligence (ONI), entered into dangerous alliances with the Mafia and held hands with Chiang Kai-shek's opium-smuggling secret police. In the post-war years the young CIA enlisted as Cold War "assets" the heroin-smuggling Corsican network and the Sicilian Mafia.

Soon the CIA was knee-deep, at the operations level, in heroin, opium, marijuana and LSD; cocaine would come later. In the '50s, fearful that the Soviets were getting a leg up on mind-control drugs, the CIA, through its notorious MK-ULTRA and MK-DELTA projects, unloaded hundreds of millions of tabs of LSD on unaware Americans, many of them university kids. In the '60s during the Vietnam War, the CIA collaborated with Southeast Asia's heroin smuggling generals and the opium-growing tribesmen of the Golden Triangle; the stories of the CIA's Air America planes taking dope to market are legend.

After the Bay of Pigs, the CIA's paramilitary anti-Castro Cubans drifted from their Miami base into major narcotics smuggling and by the '70s had developed alliances with far-right dope-financed terrorist organizations that the agency kept at arm's length but occasionally used to its advantage. In the '80s the CIA's contra re-supply network and cooperating Central American military honchos took advantage of the cocaine boom with the agency's knowledge and occasionally under its protection.

Through all these years there was, as Nixon once memorably put it, "a lot of hanky panky" between the CIA and its underworld assets and allies, many of whom were importing increasing amounts of heavy drugs into America. The CIA's method in these alliances was to hold its soiled cards close to its vest and, when a drug-dealing asset was caught by the cops, intercede with the law. Scores of major narcotics cases were dropped at CIA insistence during the 1970s.

Intimately and subtly involved in a "lot of hanky panky" for more than three decades has been the fine hand of George Bush: in the early 60's as a CIA operative; in the late 70's as its director; and as Reagan's drug czar in the 80's; and in the 90's as commander in chief.

Through the years inestimable billions of dollars confiscated from drug trading has flowed the world over to pay for secretive and illegal operations unauthorized by Congress — the Middle East and Central America, to name two. From Nixon to Bush, the GOP, through corrupt activities, built the largest campaign warchests in the political history of the United States.

The Agency was so effective at protecting its contra-resupply narco-traffickers during the '80s that two assistant U.S. attorneys in Miami in charge of drug prosecutions, R. Jerome Stanford and Richard Gregorie, resigned in frustration because of Agency stonewalling and deep-sixing of evidence. Gregorie told a Senate subcommittee that the CIA's lack of cooperation in drug prosecutions amounted to a "constitutional crisis."

Far from dragging its heels in the past about drug wars as the *Times* reported, the CIA has plunged into the fray but with disastrous results. When Nixon first declared war against drugs in October in 1969 and made the CIA the chief drug intelligence agency, the result was that by 1971 more than 100 CIA-trained Cuban exiles, under cover of narcotics enforcement, were functioning as a White House goon squad; that experiment terminated in Watergate.

BUNCIN/DEACON, the CIA's major experiment in drug interdiction, *increased* the flow of drugs into the country. So has every other CIA attempt to help out the drug wars. When George Bush was CIA director in 1976, he received two reports, one from the DEA, the other from the General Accounting Office, evaluating the CIA's sad-sack role in the drug wars. Both concluded that drug enforcement and intelligence were two different worlds; it was folly to throw the CIA, whose business was covert operations based on maintaining unsavory alliances, into drug wars.

Bush nevertheless did just that when he became anti-drug czar in the Reagan administration. In 1983 he announced a major effort against drugs to increase "CIA help in the crackdown." The results were, once again, calamity.

DEA officials later testified before Congress that the CIA sandbagged them on Gen. Noriega, to whom the DEA sent "attaboy" letters of congratulations on his anti-drug efforts while the CIA knew the Medellín cartel was using Panama for a parking lot.

Given the agency's narcotic past, President Bush's decision to send a "reluctant" CIA once more into the breach is anything but an exercise in cost-efficiency. The CIA's role is likely to be nothing more than making sure the troops in Bush's expanded drug wars don't go off in right field and arrest the wrong people.[1]

The author has concluded that the CIA is not the model of decorous behavior for the silent services that he once considered it. The whole story including the abuse of secrecy by some intelligence officials he believes were privately profiting from the CIA-sync Asian drug traffic would "just about destroy the agency if an honest investigation were held," said the biographer of Intrepid.

As Cold War adventurism was given primacy in American foreign policy over the goals of the war on drugs, covert action and the secrets of the CIA's continuing wars in Southeast Asia were considered more important than efforts to release POWs. The POW issue has never been popular with American liberals who otherwise rush to question the CIA because it was an issue which became a cause of the American right.

One of the loudest critics of government cover-ups of POW

---

1   Warren Hinckle, "CIA protects drug traffickers," *San Francisco Examiner*, June 21, 1990.

information is Senator Jessie Helms. Ronald Reagan embraced the cause by appointing Texas billionaire Ross Perot to investigate the fate of Vietnam MIAs. But Perot took the assignment more seriously than the Reagan-Bush administration apparently intended.

When he got hard evidence of at least some POWs still alive in Southeast Asia and found his search for them blocked by American intelligence officials involved in drug trafficking, Perot complained to Vice President Bush. As soon as Bush realized where Perot was coming from, Perot was dropped like a hot stone by the administration.

With Perot's unannounced entry into the 1992 presidential race, his relationship with Bush in the 80's has exploded into major political fireworks, as this book went to press.

The Reagan-Bush ticket was elected in 1980 with no small assistance from former CIA agents who used the tricks of their trade to destabilize President Jimmy Carter's re-election campaign. They stole his debate briefing book, painted his brother Billy as a cheerleader for Libya, and planted moles in the National Security Council as well as the White House Situation Room to spy on Carter.

One of Bush's helpers in the 1980 campaign was Stefan Halper, who was not a CIA agent but had linked with the intelligence community when he married the daughter of Ray Cline, of the CIA.

A former deputy director of the spy agency and the CIA's man in Taiwan for many years, Cline organized "Agents for Bush" to boost the former CIA director's 1980 presidential run and placed his son-in-law as Bush's research chief. Halper rolled over into the Reagan-Bush campaign when the Great Communicator chose Bush as his running mate at the urging of his campaign manager, William Casey, a close friend of Bush's father.

Casey became Reagan's CIA director and architect of the Iran-contra affair. Casey pushed for Bush because he knew he came from good spook stock: George's father, former Connecticut senator and Skull and Bones man Prescott Bush, was in Army Intelligence during World War I and co-founded with Casey a right-wing think tank in 1962, the National Strategy Information Center, which used clandestine CIA funds to publish anti-left tracts. When Bush was elected president in 1988, the center had a major policy input into the new administration.

George Bush's war against drugs has been characterized by the realization that there are exceptions. Stefan Halper is an instructive figure because he represents a bridge between the first two phases of George Bush's leadership in that oft-proclaimed battle against drugs.

Phase One: 1971-77. Bush is brought into the War on Drugs by Richard Nixon and appointed to the White House Cabinet Committee on International Narcotic Control. Nixon uses the war on drugs as cover to set up the White House plumbers and other hijinks that end in Watergate, while the CIA uses the opportunity to put its agents into deep cover in the DEA and taste the forbidden fruit of domestic operations. There are assassination plots, wide-scale electronic eavesdropping and CIA-favored drug traffickers are given a certain immunity to operate as long as they do the agency's bidding. There are also indications of a wink and a nod for traffickers bringing drugs into the United States who financially support Latin American death squads that murder leftists by the thousands.

In the mid-'70s, Congress and the Justice Department attempted to crack down on the CIA covert operatives known endearingly as "cowboys," but Bush as CIA director from 1976 through 1977 blocked and stonewalled every investigation, leaving the cowboys unscathed.

1977-80 Jimmy Carter's CIA director, Adm. Stansfield Turner, purges the cowboys in the worst bloodletting in agency history: more than 800 covert operators are fired. Even Gen. Noriega is taken off the payroll.

Phase Two: 1980-1988. The angry cowboys sign up in droves for the Bush-for-President, then the Reagan-Bush campaign in 1980 and help defeat Carter by doing to his campaign what the CIA did to Allende's Chile.

Reagan begins his holy war against the Sandinistas, and Bush is put in charge of the War Against Drugs and the War Against Terrorism. The cowboys enjoy a magnificent restoration.

The CIA's airlines begin to fly again; the Miami station, which had fallen into decline after being the biggest spy post in the world during the anti-Castro plots of the '60s, is retrofitted — even Noriega is put back on the payroll; and in the name of helping the contras, the inevitable exceptions to the crackdown on drug traffickers are made. The War on Drugs again becomes a cover for the unseemly details of pursuing foreign policy goals.

Phase Three: 1989-present. George Bush's militarization of the War on Drugs. It may be too easy to tell where this is going, but all indications to date are for business as usual.

The coefficient of the War on Drugs is the War on Terrorism. The two were intertwined in the 1980s when George Bush headed both efforts. On Bush's watch, the FBI conducted its largest political surveillance operation since the tumultuous '60s, opening files on more than 19,500 opponents of U.S. policies in El Salvador and Nicaragua. The FBI bowed to Oliver North's wishes and let the Bureau be misused in a sleazy attempt to smear Jack Terrell as a "terrorist." Terrell was the first major witness to drug trafficking by the contras and their sugar daddies.

Then-Vice President Bush, as head of the Task Force on Combatting Terrorism and the Reagan Administration's executive in charge of the war on drugs, allowed the tactics of counter terrorism, the politics of the drug wars and the activities of the contra support network to become indistinguishable.

The war against terrorism and the war on drugs have similar *modi operandi* in their disdain for the Constitution. Only one career government man has the distinction of simultaneously overseeing both these "wars," George Bush.

From 1982 on, George Bush worked closely with Oliver North developing anti-terrorism and drug-wars tactics that utilized many of the same individuals in the contra-support network who provided the FBI with the names of "terrorists" to investigate.

North came up with a plan to suspend the Constitution. Bush helped the Anti-Drug Abuse Act of 1988, which brushed aside constitutional niceties to increase the government's surveillance powers over anyone suspected of drugging. Next time around, the FBI won't need to use terrorism as an excuse.[2]

During Bush's press conference in Europe with the other heads of state, he singled out the cooperation of the Eli Lilly company in opening pharmaceutical drug commerce with the Soviet Union. It should be pointed out that George Bush has been an outspoken opponent of marijuana. During Bush's terms as CIA director and drug task force chief, the volume of drugs smuggled into this country rose by 1000%.

Bob Martinez, after he was defeated for re-election as Florida's governor in 1990, was picked as Bush's drug czar. From sources in Tampa, the author learned that Martinez was under investigation for his alleged role in smuggling operations, but Thornburgh, Bush's handpicked Attorney General, removed the Assistant U.S. Attorney in Tampa before indictments came down.

The *Orlando, Florida Sentinel* published a series of articles listing the vast number of political appointees by Bush and Martinez to the czar's staff. The newspaper reported that 40% of Martinez' staff was political appointees. The average percentage of political appointees in the federal government is 10%, *The Sentinel* said.

After leaving the CIA in 1977, George Bush was made director of the Eli Lilly pharmaceutical company by none other than Dan Quayle's father and family, who owned controlling interest in the Lilly company and the *Indianapolis Star*. The entire Bush family were large stockholders in Lilly, Abbott,

---

2   Hinckle, "Bush oversaw FBI's domestic spying," *S.F. Examiner,* October 18, 1990.

Bristol and Pfizer, etc.

After Bush's disclosure of assets in 1979, it became public that Bush's family still has a large interest in Pfizer and substantial stock in the drug companies. In fact, Bush actively lobbied illegally both within and without the administration as Vice President in 1981 to permit drug companies to dump more unwanted, obsolete or especially domestically-banned substances on Third World countries.

While Vice President, Bush continued to illegally act on behalf of pharmaceutical companies by going to the IRS for special tax breaks for certain drug companies manufacturing in Puerto Rico.

In 1981, Bush was ordered to stop lobbying the IRS on behalf of the drug companies by the U.S. Supreme Court. He did, but the pharmaceutical companies still received a 23% additional tax break for their companies in Puerto Rico who make these American-outlawed drugs for sale to Third World countries!

The presidential campaign of George Bush was being seriously damaged before it had begun. On top of persistent accusations that he was party to the whole Iran-Contra arms and hostages scandal, there were new allegations that he may have known of, and acquiesced in, drug deals with Latin American gangsters as part of the contras package.

The story, which first emerged during hearings by the Senate subcommittee directed by John Kerry of Massachusetts, is that planes taking arms to Central America in the early days of the illicit provision of arms to the contras, returned to the U.S. loaded with cocaine.

The trade, so the allegations go, was organized by the notorious Medellín cartel in Colombia and took in America's current public enemy number one, General Manuel Antonio Noriega.

One of Bush's assistants, Donald Gregg, was allegedly the Washington contact for the operation, known as the Arms Supermarket. Gregg has denied the accusation. Bush has come in, both through his relationship with Gregg, and through his former role as Director of the CIA, whose members were tied up in the contra operation.

A much more direct involvement was also alleged during the subcommittee hearings. The most significant witness was Ramon Milian Rodriguez, now serving a long jail sentence for laundering hundreds of millions of dollars for the Medellín cartel. Milian claims that the cartel allocated a little under $10 million to the contras, and that the man who distributed it was Felix Rodriguez. "I was led to believe he was reporting directly to Vice-President Bush."

The further allegation is that a member of the staff of General Noriega, the Panamanian leader indicted for massive drug dealings in the U.S., arranged the purchase of arms for the contras through an Israeli network. The staff member was Michael Harari, a "former" member of the Israeli Mossad.

He organized the transport of weapons from Yugoslavia and Eastern Europe to Panama. In exchange for this service, cocaine brought to Panama from Colombia, was forwarded to air strips in Costa Rica or Honduras being used for the arms deliveries. The planes took the coke on to the United States.

These, and other incriminating matters have been emerging piecemeal. They were highlighted in a television report by Leslie Cockburn, author of *Out of Control*, a study linking the contras to the drug trade. The book also implicates the gang of four (Admiral Poindexter, Lt. Col. Oliver North, Gen. Richard Secord and Albert Hakim) who set up the Iran-contra deal. Gen. Secord has sued Cockburn for libel.

Iran-contra and its ramifications should have been featured prominently in the presidential election campaign. The question put to every witness during the Watergate crisis 15 years ago applies to Bush: what did he know about the Iran-contra affair, and when did he know it? Bush's opponents say that, if he did not know, he was incompetent, and if he did, he is now lying. Bush refused to say what advice he offered Reagan, claimed he did not realize it was a swap of arms for hostages, and that he never knew that arms were being shipped to the contras.

Secretary of State George Schultz said Bush attended a meeting at which Schultz and then-Secretary of Defense, Caspar Weinberger, argued with the President over the propriety of selling arms to the Ayatollah. Bush denies it.

It has been established that two of Bush's senior advisers, Donald Gregg and Col. Samuel Watson, were in contact with one of the men organizing the illegal dispatch of arms to the contras, Felix Rodriguez. Gregg and Watson say Rodriguez never told them about the deliveries, and certainly never discussed it with Bush.

Gregg is a former CIA officer who met Bush when he was the agency's director. Rodriguez is also a former CIA man, an intimate friend of Gregg, and met Bush on a number of occasions while he [Rodriguez] was sending arms over the border into Nicaragua.

A memo setting the agenda for one of those meetings states that its purpose was to discuss "resupply of the contras." Col. Watson says the memo was typed wrong. The secretary who typed it says she wrote just what Col. Watson dictated.

In the summer of 1986, Bush visited Israel. The Israeli official most closely involved in the hostage negotiations with the Iranians discussed it with him. His chief of staff, Craig Fuller, wrote a memo of the discussion. Bush now says that he did not then have enough information to understand what he was being told, so he did not realize that arms were being traded for hostages.

In his autobiography, *Looking Forward*, Bush gives the impression that he hardly knew Marine Lt. Col. Ollie North. Publicly, on Iran-contra, Bush has insisted that he was "out of the loop" on North's ill-fated arms-for-hostages dealing with Iran and the baksheesh of guns for the contras.

Bush's bad-relative treatment of North was somewhat ungenerous, since North in his testimony before the Iran-contra committee hailed Bush's bravery in reading the riot act to the death squads when North and Bush visited El Salvador together in 1983.

The Marine came close to tears in reciting how the veep was one of the few people in the Reagan administration to console him when his father died. Despite these public suggestions of intimacy, the committee remained uncurious about the Bush-North relationship. It passed up fertile ground.

Now the Bush and North connection is revealed with the 2,600 uncensored pages of North's White House diaries released in May and June under a Freedom of Information lawsuit filed by the National Security Archives in Washington, D.C., and Ralph Nader's *Public Citizen*. The unmistakable conclusion to be drawn from the copious entries in North's notebooks is that Ollie North and Bush were as close as the stamp to the envelope.

North was keenly interested in the Vice President's travel schedule. Whenever Bush went abroad, North would make a note of it and hit up the head of the country Bush was visiting for aid to the contras. Whether Bush actually made such solicitations himself is not indicated in North's hen-scratchy shorthand. But specific diary entries which were either partially blacked out or deleted entirely from the redacted version of the diaries released by the Iran-contra committee show Bush performing a variety of tasks for North.

In September 1985, shortly after the first Israeli-arranged shipment of U.S. TOW missiles to Iran, Bush met with Israeli spy Amiram Nir in Israel. Nir, who died in a mysterious plane crash in Mexico in 1988, was a key player in the arms shipment to Iran and the "diversion" of funds from the overpriced Iranian arms to the contras.

This meeting may have been the embryo of the diversion scheme. (An aborted Senate Intelligence Committee report on the Iran-contra affair in January 1987 deleted a reference to the Bush-Nir meeting at the request of the Reagan White House; the entire report was then withheld on a 7-6 committee vote and remains classified.)

Bush met with Nir a second time on July 29, 1986, in Jerusalem. His aide Craig Fuller took detailed notes of the briefing Nir gave Bush on the arms-for-hostages progress, or lack thereof. A diary entry shows that Bush met with North in Washington on Aug. 6, the day he returned from Israel, and gave him Fuller's notes. Yet Bush has repeatedly said he knew nothing of the arms schemes until December 1986.

Observers of the Iran-contra affair who have compared the uncensored North diaries with the edited and blacked-out partial version used by the joint committee note that many of the deletions were references to Bush. This is consistent with press reports that the committee, once it hastened to determine that there were no grounds to recommend the impeachment of Reagan, wanted to wind up its inquiry quickly and did not want to track the activities of the Vice President.

North's diaries reveal that the committee was not independent. The *Tampa Tribune* reported July 1, 1990 that a North notebook entry showed that on March 4, 1985, North and then National Security Adviser McFarlane met with four Republican representatives to discuss the congressional ban on aiding the contras by seeking contributions from third countries such as Saudi Arabia.

Two of the congressmen present, Reps. Henry Hyde of Illinois and Bill McCollum of Florida, went on to become North's staunchest defenders on the Iran-contra committee. Other entries showed that McCollum's aide Vaughn Forrest worked directly with North on resupplying the contras.

In one entry North tells Forrest, "Secord running guns to Iran." The *Tribune* reported that McCollum's aide toured contra camps in Costa Rica with North's aide Rob Owen during the time when the contra resupply effort was being partially coordinated out of the Vice President's office. At this writing, Forrest is running for Congress in a newly created district in Florida.

According to the Kerry report of the Senate Foreign Relations Subcommittee on Terrorism and Narcotics, there was "obvious and widespread" drug trafficking by contra suppliers going on in the war zones of northern Costa Rica. The Kerry committee found that these drugs-for-guns activities were covered up by CIA operatives and other players in the resupply network.

In 1986, when many of the Bush diary entries were being logged, Ollie North was working out of a secret office provided by the Vice President when Bush headed the task Force on Combatting Terrorism. (North had previously worked with his secretary Fawn Hall in 1983-84 for the "Crisis Management Center" chaired by Bush.) It was here that the inventive North developed his plan to suspend the Constitution, about which Iran-contra committee member Jack Brooks of Texas was attempting to question him when he was cut off by the committee chairman, Sen. Daniel Inouye (D-Hawaii).

Bush's terrorism task force created a new "Office to Combat Terrorism," which North headed. The office was kept secret from some members of the National Security Council. Two Bush aides who worked on the task force, Robert Earl and Craig Coy, moved in to give North a hand. Earl's deposition to the Iran-contra committee indicates that much of the work they did was on Iranian arms sales and contra resupply.

The North-Bush story has yet to be fully probed in the Iran-contra committee, or at North's trial. North got a new trial after a federal appeals court determined that evidence used against him had been tainted by the immunized testimony he gave to the Iran-contra committee. Independent prosecutor Lawrence M. Walsh could still ask North about his relationship with Bush in all its aspects. The backsliding Congress could not immunize testimony it was afraid to hear.[3]

On May 15, 1984, George Bush, then vice president, visited Pakistan. He was the first ranking U.S. official to come to Islamabad since 1977.

---

3   Hinckle, "Secret links between Bush and North," *S.F. Examiner*, July 26, 1990.

Gen. Zia's gratitude knew few bounds, and the Vice President was treated as royalty. At a magnificent state banquet, Bush rose to acknowledge the applause of the Pakistani generals and praised the Zia government's anti-narcotics efforts as a "personal" satisfaction to him as America's head narc.

The general beamed in self-congratulation.

When Bush left Pakistan three days later, he announced an extraordinary outpouring from the U.S. treasury: $3.2 billion in new U.S. military aid, and another $2 billion for the Pakistani army providing the arms pipeline to the CIA-supported Afghan rebels.

At the time Bush praised Pakistan's anti-drug stance, that nation was providing as much as 70 percent of the high-grade heroin entering the world market. Most of the dope came from an elite Pakistani military unit that managed the truck convoys carrying the CIA's arms to Afghanistan, touted as the largest CIA "covert op" since the early days of the Vietnam War.

The truck company, owned by the Army, was the largest transportation business in Pakistan. The trucks left for Afghanistan laden with arms and returned laden with poppies. The fabulous profits were spread throughout the military hierarchy.

Pakistan's role in transporting raw opium gum from Afghanistan and processing it in laboratories in southwest Pakistan was well known in the European intelligence community. It was also known to the DEA and the CIA. The question is how could then-Vice President Bush, a former CIA director, who as head of the National Narcotics Border Interdiction System was privy to world-wide narcotics intelligence, not know what was happening in Pakistan?

Why would he be instrumental in rewarding such a dope-pushing regime with $5 billion in military aid? Was the Vice President naive, or did he know too much, or was he just following orders? Once again the good lieutenant?

How indeed could the State Department, CIA and DEA look the other way on heroin profiteering by our allies when Bush's drug czar, William Bennett, was asking Americans to surrender some of their basic constitutional rights, including the right not to be unreasonably searched, in the name of the war against drugs?

And what sort of answers could be given now that the primary apology of the past — that Cold War realities had to take precedence over drug war tactics — was old business?

The answers tell a lot about the hypocrisy of American foreign policy, but divulge more about the President, the only figure in public life who has been in the drug wars of three administrations beginning with Nixon in the early 1970s.

Since the Nixon years, both the rubric and the machinery of the "war against drugs" have been used for purposes other than stopping the flow of drugs. It has been used to conceal intelligence operations, to conceal covert action and foreign policy failures, and as a front for counter-insurgency adventures in other countries, and for bringing in cash for campaign expenses.

Although the kindest explanation for Bush's passivity to the Afghan rebel-Pakistani drug connection would be naiveté, the President is not naive. He seems able to put on an air of naiveté like a protective vest when facing battering, embarrassing questions from the press.

Bush also has unappreciated skills much like a snake-oil salesman. When the President announced his war on drugs to the nation from the Oval Office in 1990, he held up for the national television audience a bag of crack cocaine he said had been purchased in Lafayette Park, across the street from the White House.

When the bust of the crack dealer turned out to be a set-up and a phony, Bush momentarily lost his cool and testily asked inquiring reporters whose side they were on: the President, or some "drug guy."

The nation's many wars against drugs have been used to distract Americans from other realities of politics. The fact that George Bush began his third term in the war on drugs with a lie, points up the consistency of his political lifestyle. [4]

The concept that the military can win a war on drugs is also a fantasy, although a useful one for the Pentagon. A Department of Defense report says that a 24-hour surveillance of the Florida-to-California border would require: a third of the Navy's fleet, more radar planes than the United States has, deployment of as many as 100 battalions, and cost a billion dollars a year — and that's only the southern border of the nation.

The militarizing of the war on drugs puts Bush higher in the saddle of a white horse he has been riding for almost 20 years — the many-splendored elastic-in-purpose drug war. Bush has been involved in the war on drugs through three administrations. His baptism was in 1971 as a member of Richard Nixon's now notorious Cabinet Committee on International Narcotics Control.

This select group included such grand old names as John Mitchell and Egil Krogh and out of it grew the White House plumbers and the hydra-headed monster known as Watergate. The committee was the instrument whereby the CIA was brought into the war on drugs; drug enforcement became a matter of "national security" and national security a blanket excuse for law-breaking.

The committee also blessed the cross-over of many CIA covert-action operatives into what became the Drug Enforcement Administration. The DEA, in turn, served as a cover for illegal CIA domestic actions and brought into government service the shadowy network of anti-Castro Cubans left over from the Bay of Pigs invasion — men primed for crime and violence.

In Bush's early days in the drug wars, the policy now operative in Peru that anti-drug efforts are anti-leftist guerrilla efforts was formulated. Through the years since, Bush never turned his sights on the commingling of rightist death squads and drug profits, particularly in Latin America, and developed a

---

4   Hinckle, "Afghan drug traffic escapes Bush's notice," *S.F. Examiner*, May 17, 1990.

masterful ability to see only what he wants to see.[5]

There are degrees of subtlety in photo opportunities. Some are flagrant public relations, as was the photo op staged on Jan. 4, 1984, in the Florida keys. Bush, then head of the Vice Presidential Joint Florida Drug Task Force Group, mugged for the cameras with his good buddy of 10 years, speedboat king Don Arnow, builder of the cigarette boat, an ocean-going Ferrari that was the world's fastest and sleekest powerboat.

Arnow had invented a 39-foot catamaran he called "Blue Thunder." Bush was anxious to test it on a simulated drug patrol for the media, racing along the southeastern Florida coastline favored by drug smugglers. A White House photographer followed Bush in a helicopter in case the press missed a dramatic shot of Bush against the sea.

Afterwards, Bush told the press that Customs should purchase boats like Blue Thunder. "Boats like that would help in the drug war."

Not surprisingly, Arnow's company, USA Racing Team, won the government contract in 1985 to manufacture pursuit boats for the Vice President's drug-interdiction group. In 1986, Arnow's company was again awarded the contract to manufacture the pursuit craft of the War on Drugs despite the fact that the Blue Thunders were widely considered a joke in North Miami's speedboat industry: they were always in the shop with ailments and were incredibly slow next to the powerful models the drug traffickers used.

Arnow was the odds-on favorite to get the contract again for 1987 until a mob hit man killed him in his white Mercedes on North Miami's "Thunderboat Alley," a dead-end street where the world's most powerful speedboats are built.

Arnow sold his boats to the rich and powerful: Spain's King Juan Carlos, King Hussein of Jordan, Charles Keating of Lin-

---

5   Hinckle, "Another Vietnam brewing in Peru?" *S.F. Examiner*, May 24, 1990.

coln Savings and Loan, and George Bush of Kennebunkport.

He also sold them to major mobsters and international drug traffickers. Arnow began by building boats with disguised extra fuel tanks to carry cocaine and accepted payment in bags of cash.

A new investigative book, *Blue Thunder*, describes how Arnow developed into an indentured servant of the mob who did what he was told with no questions asked and became involved in Mafia drug-smuggling operations ranging from the Meyer Lansky organization to the Purple Gang of the Genovese crime family.

Thomas Burdick and Charlene Mitchell, authors of *Blue Thunder*, report that Arnow was so close to the Purple Gang's Frankie "Pizza-furter" Viserto that in 1981 he wrote a letter to the feds on Frankie's behalf offering this "boating and fishing enthusiast" employment as a boat demonstrator providing the "federales" would let him out of the penitentiary where he was sentenced for heroin smuggling.

Arnow's association with the notorious Mafioso drug smuggler and gun runner began in the early '70s about the same time he became friends with George Bush. They were parallel but not intermingled friendships.

"While Viserto was gaining control of the largest heroin-smuggling ring in the country, Bush was climbing the Washington political ladder. As Arnow became more deeply enmeshed in mafia-sponsored drug activities, he clinched a multimillion-dollar government contract. Ultimately by awarding Arnow the Blue Thunder contract, Bush allowed not one, but two, drug-smuggling arms of the mob to penetrate the government's anti-drug program," the authors write.

Bush and Arnow were such good friends that a few weeks before he was murdered in February 1987, Arnow told his wife that if anything happened to him and she had problems, she should call the Vice President in Washington. Mrs. Arnow took over the company after her husband's mob-style execution and called Bush with a question: "Should she go to Panama to see

Gen. Manuel Noriega about some Blue Thunder boats the general had ordered?"

"He told me that there were a lot of bad things going on with that guy and that I shouldn't have anything to do with him," she said. Bush has insisted that until the 1987 indictments of Noriega for drug smuggling, he thought the dictator was our loyal ally.

The question of how Bush, a former CIA director and general in the war on drugs, could be so close to a man with such major mob connections is as confounding as how Bush was about the last person to discover that Noriega was a drug trafficker. The answers lead to cynicism about the war on drugs.[6]

Some of the documents you sent to us are almost illegible.

From our review of Agency materials, we know that good copies could have been provided.

**Richard Thornburgh's testy note
to George Bush's CIA, 1976**

Attorney General Richard Thornburgh had cut a deal. The federal government would front Panamanian narco-dictator Manuel Antonio Noriega's multimillion-dollar legal fees in return for the jailed despot's attorneys withdrawing subpoenas for Noriega's CIA payroll stubs.

But Miami Federal District Court Judge William Hoeveler ruled that the Criminal Justice Act that permits the government to finance the defense of indigent defendants could not be stretched to convenience Noriega's pricey $250 to $300-an-hour attorneys.

The former Panamanian ruler is known to be filthy rich but the U.S. government has put liens on all of his known bank accounts. The arrangement presented to the court by

---

6   Hinckle, "George Bush and the speedboat king," *S.F. Examiner,* December 13, 1990.

Thornburgh's Justice Department would have had the taxpayers advance the cost of his defense for a promissory note signed by the imprisoned general.

Had the deal not been aborted, Thornburgh might have kept sealed the secret records of Noriega's business relationship with U.S. intelligence since he began to inform on Panamanian leftists in the Eisenhower administration.

And Thornburgh's boss, President Bush, would have been revealed as one of the paymasters of the narco-general.

When he headed the CIA in 1976, Bush so valued Noriega as an agency "asset" that he rebuffed attempts to sever the dope-dealing militarist's ties with the CIA. At the time, Noriega had been caught bribing American GIs in Panama to provide him National Security Agency electronic surveillance tapes of Panamanian politicians.

According to a recent book on Noriega, the general continued in his $100,000-a-year CIA arrangement. That figure rose to a reported $200,000 a year during the Reagan-Bush administration.

Governmental secrecy has been an over-abiding concern of Bush: "When I took over as DCI (Director of Central Intelligence), there were daily messages from CIA stations on my desk every morning reporting that we were losing valuable sources of information as a result of worldwide publicity caused by leaks from irresponsible investigators on Capitol Hill," he wrote in his autobiography.

Thornburgh, as Attorney General, has served Bush well in this regard. He put an effective national-security collar on the independent prosecutor in the Iran-contra investigation, and blocked the criminal prosecution of Joseph Fernandez, the former CIA station chief in Costa Rica during Iran-Contra, by invoking a 1980 law that gives the Attorney General power to withhold classified information in national-security trials. Independent Counsel Lawrence Walsh accused Thornburgh of creating "fictional secrets."

It was not always so with Thornburgh. In 1976, when

Thornburgh headed the criminal division of the Justice Department under Ford and Bush was director of the CIA, Thornburgh pushed Bush to release CIA records involving more than 100 CIA and DEA agents for offenses ranging from padding expense accounts to plotting assassinations.

When Bush took over the CIA in 1976 (reportedly he barely beat out then-Solicitor General Robert H. Bork and Supreme Court Justice Byron White) the agency was on the ropes after the mid-70s revelations of share-rental assassination plots with the Mafia and illegal domestic spying on "radlibs."

Thornburgh led Justice's prosecution of former CIA Director Helms for perjury before Congress in the CIA-manipulated overthrow of the Allende government in Chile. Thornburgh accused Bush of stalling and deleting documents he had requested. (Bush was so cavalier as to write Helms and warn him, against Justice Department admonitions, of the CIA case forming against him.)

When Bush's stonewalling took the form of sending illegible copies of documents to Justice, a piqued Thornburgh asked the Ford White House to order Bush to produce good copies.

CIA Director Bush was most interested in killing a Justice Department report, also in Thornburgh's jurisdiction, about serious wrongdoing in 1972-1975 by CIA agents operating in the Drug Enforcement Agency. Bush's political mentor, President Nixon, appointed him in 1971 to the White House Cabinet Committee on International Narcotics Control, which made Bush knowledgeable about the War on Drugs used as a cover for political warfare.

The controversial 1975 report was called the DeFeo Report, after one of its authors. It was a hot item in Washington because it detailed drug dealings by Panamanian officials, including the CIA's man, Noriega and an assassination plot against Noriega by DEA/CIA cowboys.

Right-wing congressmen were anxious to lay hands on the DeFeo Report as a vehicle to sabotage negotiations with the

Panamanian government over the Panama canal. But they were stonewalled by Thornburgh, earning him Bush's gratitude despite their public spats.

The issue of Thornburgh withholding the Panama drug report from Congress came up during his 1988 confirmation hearings as Reagan's "Mr. Clean" Attorney General nominee to replace the muddied Meese.

Thornburgh, who had written a memorandum about keeping the DeFeo secrets from Congress, assured congressmen that he would give them the Justice Department report quickly. He never did.

Last month Thornburgh became the first attorney general to take a lie-detector test while in office. Thornburgh took the test voluntarily as part of an internal Justice Department investigation into leaks to the media. He passed easily.

Obviously, anyone who has helped George Bush cover up drug-war secrets for so many years has little to fear from a polygraph.[7]

---

7   Hinckle, "Thornburgh joins drug-secrets game," *S.F. Examiner*, May 30, 1990.

CHAPTER 7

"Out of the Loop"

"National Security has become a synonym for coverup. Reagan didn't know, Bush denied, Casey died, Poindexter lied, Ollie was tried, and Noriega fried, all while patriots for profit made millions from the Iran-Contra, Panama, and Gulf War. It's time to stop the "Bushlip!"

James "Bo" Gritz, war hero, author,
and Presidential candidate

"...the United States Government is inherently and operationally incapable of developing and successfully carrying out clandestine operations, primarily because they run at total opposites to our basic way of life.

L. Fletcher Prouty in *The Secret Team: The CIA and Its Allies in Control of the United States and the World*

Hours after being sentenced to two years probation for perjury in the Iran-contra scandal on January 24, 1990, retired Air Force Maj. Gen. Richard Secord said that a "cowardly" former President Reagan "has been hiding out" to avoid accounting for his participation.

Secord, the middleman, did not receive jail time or a fine for lying to congressional investigators about buying former White House aide Oliver L. North a $13,800 home-security system.

Secord told a news conference that he believed Reagan "was well aware" of the "general outlines" of the covert operation involving secret arms sales to Iran and clandestine assistance to

Nicaraguan rebels.

He claimed that Reagan "should have stood up and taken the heat right at the time the disclosures started coming out" more than four years ago. Secord claimed that the plan was a presidential directive, regardless of how much Reagan knew about its specifics.

"The diversion was a small portion of a large, difficult, dangerous covert operation on which Reagan was briefed regularly," he said. He added that two former national security advisers, John M. Poindexter and Robert C. McFarlane, and the late CIA director William J. Casey, all had assured him Reagan was kept informed of the operation.

Richard Brenneke, a self-professed contract operative for the CIA, recounted to reporters Frank Snepp (himself a former CIA agent), Jonathan King, and to the Senate Foreign Relations Committee, that from 1983 on, Bush's office had been a "control point" for contra-supply operations by Israeli agents out of Panama, Honduras and El Salvador. He fingered Bush's then-national-security adviser, Don Gregg, as ringmaster, and Felix Rodriguez as a principal field operative. He even implicated himself, saying that as a contract pilot he had flown drugs to the United States as part of the increasingly corrupt U.S.-Israeli supply shuttle.

Some sources told Snepp and King that Brenneke was an Israeli intelligence plant trying to discredit former Israeli Prime Minister Shimon Peres and other Laborites in Tel Aviv who had embroiled Israel in the Iran-Contra scandal. When ABC's *World News Tonight* broadcast three circumspect accounts of his allegations in spring 1988, the White House savaged his credibility, tagging him falsely as an indicted co-conspirator in a New York gun-running case.

A year later, after Bush's election, the Justice Department brought perjury charges against Brenneke, alleging that he lied about his affiliation with the CIA (he'd said he had one) and an early episode in the Iran-contra affair. By the time he was finally cleared of all charges last May, his reputation had been so sullied by mudslinging that neither the press nor Congress could be persuaded to re-examine what he had said. Killing the messenger had been raised to a fine art.

The real significance of Brenneke's case is how it ties in Bush. During the 1989 trial of Oliver North the government released a 42-page condensation of classified documents that thrust Bush to the very center of Contragate.

More recently, two Washington-based organizations, the National Security Archive and Public Citizen, have used the Freedom of Information Act to pry loose previously suppressed portions of North's diaries that damage what's left of Bush's deniability.

To appreciate these revelations and Bush's cover-up you have to recall what he and his former aides have said about their role in Contragate. Don Gregg, who once headed the Vice President's National Security Staff, declared flatly: "We never discussed the contras. We had no responsibility for it [the contra war]. We had no expertise in it." Bush insisted that he knew nothing of the "privatized" supply initiative until it became front-page news in late 1986, *after* the congressional ban on contra aid had eased.

Given the new historical record, it's now clear that we were Bush-whacked: The "privatized" aid network Bush allegedly knew nothing about never really existed anyway. What's more, Brenneke has been proven right about the issue that so dominated the Iran-contra hearings. The "diversion" of Iran arms profits to the contras, he warned us, was never more than a decoy to draw attention away from a far darker scandal in which Bush was deeply involved.

When CIA Director Bush met Don Gregg in 1976, using third-party "cutouts" to fund unpopular causes behind Congress's back was the rage in Langley, Virginia. A year before, during the twilight of the Vietnam War, both Israel and Saudi Arabia had been encouraged to provide secret handouts to Saigon to offset U.S. aid cutbacks. Not long after Bush settled into his CIA job, two of his deputies proposed that the CIA look to private companies to front and implement sensitive operations.

As a sometime CIA liaison to Congress, Bush knew how crippling oversight by Congress could be. The answer to that, apparently, was increased deniability of the sort these cutout operations allowed.

During Reagan's first year and a half in office, cutouts and indirect funding became operational staples at Casey's newly "revitalized" CIA, and basic tools in its burgeoning secret war against the Sandinista government in Nicaragua.

In July 1982, Gregg, then an intelligence specialist on the National Security Council, drew up a "finding," to be signed by the President, designed to give legality to such deep-cover operations.

His draft, though later overlooked by Iran-contra investigators, reads in retrospect like a blueprint for everything that would finally define Reagan's "secret war" , "funding, arms supply, and some training" by "third-country nationals," combined with supplementary aid from "selected Latin American and European governments, organizations and individuals."

The "finding" was never adopted; nobody wanted to add to the lengthening paper trail. But soon afterward, two of Gregg's old Vietnam colleagues, Rudy Enders and Felix Rodriguez, rallied him behind an impressive substitute.

Both Enders and Rodriguez had met Gregg in Vietnam in the early 1970s and had worked with him in developing a highly effective helicopter assault strategy for jungle warfare. Rodriguez was already renowned for tracking down and killing Che Guevara in 1967, and Enders studied at Gregg's elbow to become one of the CIA's top paramilitary specialists.

In 1981, he and Rodriguez, who had retired from the agency several years earlier, traveled to Central America to combat leftist insurgents more effectively. The blueprint they drew up, dubbed "Pink Team Plan," borrowed heavily from the assault strategy they had conceived in Vietnam, but with one critical difference. Whereas CIA contract pilots had flown the prescribed counterinsurgent missions there, this time Cuban exiles did the dirty work, under the ostensible sponsorship of Honduras, El Salvador and Guatemala.

In March 1983, Gregg, now elevated to the Vice President's national-security adviser, forwarded the Pink Team Plan to his colleague Robert McFarlane, who sent it to his boss, the President's NSC chief, William Clark. "This is representative of the kinds of things we can do with Israel if we work quietly behind the scenes," McFarlane wrote in a covering note that escaped notice during the Iran-contra investigations. "I set this in motion with my Israeli counterpart, David Kimche, over a year ago." Kimche was a top Israeli intelligence expert, and what he had set in motion, according to Brenneke, was a joint Israeli-U.S. paramilitary operation against the Sandinistas.

The Israelis had long been involved in Central American affairs. In the late 1970s, when the U.S. cut aid to the region's various pariah regimes, including Anastasio Somoza's Nicaraguan dictatorship, weapons merchants from Tel Aviv and Haifa picked up the slack. As the Somocistas gradually transformed into the contras in the early 1980s, Israeli entrepreneurs simply followed the market. By late 1982, the CIA, working with the Mossad, had set up a covert pipeline to the newborn contras running from arms marts in Eastern Europe through warehouses in Texas and North Carolina to bases in Costa Rica and Honduras.

In the author's version and experience there is a lot more to this.

On Friday, May 27, 1983, the *Tico Times* of San Jose, Costa Rica, under the headline "U.S. Beating Victim Back in Texas," reported that Mark Clark, "The U.S. tourist who was mugged on a Gulfito street, then apparently falsely accused of murdering a Civil Guard, viciously beaten by a group of police in the middle of the street, and held in jail for a week, is home in Houston,

Texas, sore and bitter."[1]

Many serious questions still linger about this event eight years later, but to my knowledge, there has never been any further investigation into the mugging, beating and escape of Clark from Costa Rica. The following is only a partial list of the unanswered questions which spring immediately to mind:

- Why was Clark (if that was even his real name) in Gulfito at that time, and how did he come to be mugged?
- If he had actually been victimized, why would he have been charged with murdering a Civil Guardsman?
- If he was not responsible for the death of the guardsman, what has been the disposition of the murder investigation by the Costa Rican authorities?
- Why would Clark have been beaten by other Costa Rican guards if he had himself been mugged?
- Is it possible that he was actually involved in the killing?
- How did he receive messages to learn that a hold had been listed against his name by Costa Rican immigration officials, as the article reported?
- How could he possibly have escaped from the Gulfito jail with accomplices, or was he actually under house arrest, and if so, why would that have been permitted in the case of a capital crime?
- Who else helped Clark escape?
- Why does the escapee from Costa Rica escape the scrutiny of Iran-contra Investigators?

Since Clark's escape, private individuals attempting to reconstruct the details of the event have been told by employees of the *Tico Times* that the newspaper office burned down and the original issues were lost in the fire. The replacement issues with which they were provided carried a completely different story in the section previously containing the Clark escape story by

---

1   Linda Frazier, "U.S. Beating Victim Back in Texas," *Tico Times,* May 27, 1983.

Linda Frazier. She was one of the eight journalists and contras killed in the bombing of a press conference held almost exactly one year later by Eden Pastora, the dissident former Sandinista hero, at La Penca, Nicaragua to denounce the CIA's role in the Contra war. Is it possible that the La Penca bombing, which specifically targeted journalists, was also planned to eliminate Linda Frazier?

The following is an Associated Press article:

EX-CIA OFFICIAL PLEADS INNOCENT IN IRAN-CONTRA

Alexandria, Va — The former CIA station chief in Costa Rica, Joseph Fernandez, pleaded innocent Monday to four criminal charges based on his role in the Iran-contra affair. U.S. District Judge Claude Hilton set a trial for July 10, then released Fernandez on his personal recognizance. He set May 12 for motions on how to handle classified information that may come up during the trial. An indictment filed by special prosecutor Lawrence Walsh alleges that Fernandez, who operated under the pseudonym Tomas Castillo, lied about plans to build an airstrip in Costa Rica to supply the Nicaraguan contras at the time of a congressional ban on military aid to the guerrillas. He also is charged with lying to investigators when he denied that then-White House aide Oliver North was involved in the contra supply operation.

The following are excerpts from an Associated Press story.[2]

WASHINGTON — A federal judge threw out the Iran-contra case against a former CIA station chief Friday, two days after Attorney General Dick Thornburgh barred courtroom use of classified information on CIA facilities and programs in Central America.

The information protected by an affidavit that Mr. Thornburg filed Wednesday concerns the locations of three CIA facilities,

---

2   "EX-CIA officer won't be tried — Iran-contra figure's case voided after key material withheld," *The Dallas Morning News*, November 25, 1989

*including stations in El Salvador and Honduras. The govern-
ment also refuses to allow details to surface in court about three
CIA programs in Costa Rica where Mr. Fernandez was CIA.*

*On July 24, the day Mr. Fernandez's trial was to begin,
Judge Hilton rejected a last-minute proposal by the Justice
Department and independent counsel to substitute numbers for
the CIA facilities and to drop part of one charge dealing with an
airstrip to avoid delving into the programs.*

*Mr. Fenandez was indicted on four charges, including making
false statements and obstructing inquiries into the Iran-contra
affair by the CIA inspector general and the presidentially
appointed Tower Commission.*

*The retired CIA officer call Judge Hilton's decision "wonder-
ful" but said he was troubled that CIA operatives performing
what he called legitimate duties could be subjected to political
motivation.*

Fernandez' CIA programs had the following results:

- Transcripts and witnesses were made available to the government of Costa Rica proving that ex-President José Figueras was an admitted CIA agent while president.
- Robert Vesco was allowed to remain in Costa Rica by this same ex-President, while the U.S. government allegedly had warrants for his arrest.
- "Vesco" got an offer from this same CIA-agent President that he could not refuse: To go to Cuba as CIA Station Chief and to infiltrate Castro through the "bowels" of drugs imported into the USA — guaranteed market from Robert Haynes to Costa Rica to Cuba to USA.
- The escape of Mark Clark, May 20, 1983, from Costa Rica, engineered by Russell Bowen, directed by control officer Haines.
- The initiative through ex-President Figueras to allow the exchange of arms for drugs at air strips.
- The setting up of a safe house for terrorists sympathetic to the U.S.

- The setting up of a bank with Bob White of the IRS-DUCK Operation in order to launder drug money with Panama.
- The plan to eliminate Commandante Zero (Eden Pastora).
- The plan to blow up the walls of the US embassy to help start a southern front.
- The plan to create and operate a CIA free-operating state in Costa Rica, a neutral country.

Early in the Iran-contra investigations, the Senate Intelligence Committee produced a secret report that focused on the Israeli connection. But as the hearings progressed and political sensitivities came into play, the search for culprits veered away from our most important Middle Eastern ally to less-valued scapegoats.

It was only when Brenneke stepped forward in early 1988 that suspicion swung to Jerusalem. In light of the story he told, the Pink Team Plan looked like part of a much larger scheme linking Bush's office to the deepest secret of Reagan's clandestine war.

If you believe Brenneke, Gregg became Bush's national-security adviser specifically to coordinate Israel's contra account. In fact, Brenneke claims he phoned Gregg's office repeatedly beginning in 1983 to seek instructions for Israeli supply masters.

Gregg told Frank Snepp and King that he is "morally certain" that he never talked to Brenneke, who he considers a liar, and Brenneke has not been able to document the missions he claims to have flown for the U.S.-Israeli network. Still, evidence of massive Israeli complicity in Contragate, the core of his allegations, is now persuasive.

In 1989, at North's trial, the Bush Administration cracked the window. According to its plan, in 1983, Casey proposed and retired-General Secord negotiated a joint supply venture with the Israelis known as Operation Tipped Kettle.

Under this arrangement, the Pentagon was to receive a substantial consignment of captured PLO weapons, and then pass them to the CIA for distribution. In return, the administration promised "flexibility" in meeting Israel's own financial needs, the kind of trade-off that would characterize the Reagan-Bush approach to all "third-country" support of the contras.

How much Bush's staff knew of Operation Tipped Kettle cannot be determined. But shortly after the Israeli aid spigot began to flow, the National Security Council expanded the Vice President's role in all covert operations. By the following November, according to two NSC memos available to (but never utilized by) Iran-contra investigators, the Vice President was asked routinely to "concur" in major supply shipments to the contras.

Even more, he was beginning to show up where the contras needed special friends. In December 1983, for instance, with Gregg and North in tow, Bush headed to Panama to confer with the dark angel himself, General Noriega. Israeli intelligence sources, including a Mossad operative named William Northrop, have stated that Panama was by now the switching station for Israeli supply lines reaching into Costa Rica and Honduras, and former Noriega aide José Blandon claims that his ex-boss had become a virtual protégé of the Israelis' man on the scene, former Mossad superagent Michael Harari.

To judge from official accounts, Bush and Noriega engaged in little more than diplomatic small talk, but Blandon says the get-together persuaded him to get behind the contras. Blandon's credibility has been challenged by Bush supporters, but one thing is certain. Over the next year and a half, Noriega became one of the contras' staunchest supporters.

The contras now needed all the support they could get, for U.S. aid transfusions were drying up. By spring of 1984, the CIA's audacious mining of Nicaraguan harbors had so infuriated Congress that an aid shutdown was planned, and pressure was mounting on the administration to find alternate supply sources.

In March, according to the North trial, Casey proposed another aid pitch to the Israelis (the result was Operation Tipped

Kettle II), and shortly thereafter, newly appointed national-security adviser McFarlane persuaded the Saudis to contribute $1 million a month to the contras' war chest. With that, the stage was set for what now appears to have been Bush's initiation into Contragate.

The baptism came at a White House meeting on June 25, 1984 on how to keep the contras alive. Initially, Iran-contra investigators dismissed the session as a moderately important policy review. But in light of evidence at North's trial, it appears to have been a pirate's ball. As Bush and the President looked on approvingly, Casey took the floor to argue for a radical new approach to contra resupply, including bribing countries like Honduras and Costa Rica to lend support.

According to recently declassified notes, Bush cheered Casey enthusiastically, asking at one point how anyone could object "to the U.S. encouraging third parties to provide help to the anti-Sandinistas." He worried that the administration might be seen to be trading favors for such assistance. But evidently, over the next several months, this concern faded. From a mere advocate of Casey's plan, Bush allowed himself to be converted into an active player.

The following February, with U.S. military aid now cut off, a group of senior administration officials, including North and Deputy National Security Adviser Poindexter, plotted out a battle plan for Honduras.

According to the North stipulation, they drafted a letter to Honduran President Roberto Suazo Cordova, promising him "enticements," including increased aid, if he could hop on the contras' bandwagon.

Already U.S. economic assistance to his regime had been frozen to soften him up, and in early March it paid off. Suazo said yes. On the 16th, George Bush hurried to Tegucigalpa to hand him a basket of benefits to compensate for what we had held back. Thus did the Vice President become the bagman in what amounted to an officially sanctioned extortion scheme.

Nor was Honduras the administration's only "touch." The previous August, according to recently revealed evidence, Secretary of State Schultz had proposed a similar trade-off with El Salvador, linking U.S. aid commitments there to continued support for the contras; in January, McFarlane met with President Duarte to close the deal. Though Bush wasn't directly involved, he wasn't out of it either. By early spring, Felix Rodriguez, longtime friend of his national security adviser, had become Bush's eyes and ears inside the Salvadoran military.

From the moment Contragate hit the front pages, Rodriguez was Bush's Oliver North, an inconvenient gun-bearer whose excesses threatened to backfire on the patron himself. No one could deny the two knew each other.

The public record showed that Rodriguez had met three times with the Vice President, first in January 1985, and again in May 1986, and had made over a dozen phone calls to Bush's staff. But a "chronology" released by Bush's office on the eve of the Iran-contra investigations effectively "sanitized" these contacts, implying that Rodriguez only discussed with Bush his work as a "counter-insurgency expert" in El Salvador.

Like most good cover stories, this one contained a seed of truth. From March to September 1985, Rodriguez flew about 100 combat missions against Salvadoran rebels from Ilopango airfield in El Salvador. But where Bush and his apologists played false was in casting the Salvadoran venture as unconnected with the contra war. The North stipulation makes clear that from June 1984 onward, the administration saw El Salvador as a crucial launchpad for contra supply deliveries. It's also apparent from this document that by the time Rodriguez planted himself at Ilopango, the Salvadoran regime had agreed to let the air base be used by gunrunners servicing the Resistance.

During the Iran-contra investigation, the Vice President's staff maintained that Rodriguez hadn't become involved until September 1985. But some sources allege that he was recruited into the Israeli network as early as 1983. In his recent autobiography, *Shadow Warrior*, he acknowledges that "like many of my friends in Miami, I'd been actively helping the contras since the early eighties."

Even though Bush claims he knew nothing of this, it can now be shown that he helped set up one of Rodriguez's early supply runs. As the government admitted at North's trial, Bush came up with a clever pump-primer before his trip to Honduras in March 1985. Hoping, apparently, to convince the locals that the Resistance had friends everywhere, he proposed that a private group "supportive of the Resistance" fly medical supplies to Tegucigalpa to coincide with his own arrival there. The North stipulation does not identify the private group, but in his autobiography, Rodriguez reveals that he made a supply drop as Bush was arriving.

Nor were supply deliveries Bush's only immediate concern. During the Iran-contra hearings, investigators came across an entry recording a meeting on January 23 between North and the Vice President that dealt with "CentAM C/A" (Central American covert action). No one could guess what this signified. But a passage from North's notebook shows that one "CentAm C/A" high on the lieutenant colonel's priority list in early 1985 was a planned sabotage mission inside Nicaragua involving General Noriega of Panama.

Given Bush's expanding role in covert planning, North may have briefed him on this operation. How much he may have told him cannot be determined, but on March 6, Panamanian sappers backed by British mercenaries blew up a major munitions dump in Managua.

Years later, after Noriega became a public embarrassment, Bush's defenders tried to justify our continued reliance on him by insisting that there was no "firm" intelligence in 1985 linking him to drug trafficking or anything that might have disqualified him as an ally. Again North's notebooks raise serious questions. A recently released entry reveals that at the moment of the Managua operation, Bush was complaining to other U.S. officials about narco-trafficking in Panama. *"VP distressed about drug business,"* wrote North in March 1985,

By the following summer, the taint of drugs was seeping through the entire contra supply system as contract pilots often doubled as mules for the cartel. On top of this, the press and Congress were beginning to suspect a scandal. On August 8, *The New York Times* said the contras were getting military advice from White House officials, and within days the House Intelligence Committee launched an inquiry that could hardly have gone unnoticed in the Vice President's office.

As publicity and corruption began to crimp the machinery, North and his collaborators shifted to a new tact, urging Secord to set up a supply shuttle. By September this allegedly private enterprise was taking shape so rapidly that its principals were already scouting for air bases. It was at this point that the Vice President's staff stepped into the center of the contra supply muddle.

The tip-off comes in a North diary entry dated September 10, 1985. On that day, says North, he met with Gregg and Col. James Steele, the U.S. military adviser in El Salvador, to discuss contra-related logistic problems. During the Iran-contra hearings, investigators released only a fragment of this note, a fragment so artfully censored by the White House and North's own lawyers that little could be made of it.

Its very brevity gave Gregg an excuse to deny that the meeting had taken place. That smoke screen has since evaporated. In 1988 testimony to congressional investigators, Steele confirmed the meeting *had* occurred. Though he denied having discussed the contras at that meeting, portions of North's notebooks contradict him. They also contain such a detailed account of the get-together that they cinch the case for Gregg's own complicity.

What emerges is a picture of three knowledgeable officials huddled around a conference table, weighing the merits of Ilopango over Aguacate in Honduras as a principal contra supply base. One participant (North does not say who) complained of "radar coverage" at Aguacate, and noted that contra leader Enrique Bermudez "was prepared to devote a special ops unit [to sit] astride" rebel supply lines threatening an unidentified site in El Salvador. There was also discussion of a trip by Bermudez to Ilopango "to estab[lish] log[istics] support/maint[enance]."

The September 10 meeting, with Gregg front and center, apparently hastened the contra resupply overhaul, for soon afterward the pieces fell into place. On Steele's advice, North decided to enlist Rodriguez' services, and on September 30, as Rodriguez admitted at the Iran-contra hearings, he called North to tell him "it was a go." In his testimony, Rodriguez neglected to say that he also placed a call to Gregg that day, but Gregg's own phone logs, obtained in a 1988 lawsuit, confirm that he did. They also reflect a call from North, suggesting that everybody with a stake in Secord's new setup was now gabbing openly about it.

Over the next few weeks, Secord and company geared up for their first major supply run. In late November, North, now heavily preoccupied with Iran arms shipments, accepted their help in completing a botched Israeli weapons delivery to Iran.

Bush later denied any knowledge of this, but only a couple days after Secord helped make good on the delivery, the Vice President sent a Thanksgiving note to North commending him for his "tireless work with the hostage thing and Central America."

Some see this note, which was glossed over at the Iran-contra hearings, as definitive proof of Bush's full complicity. But an even stronger clue might be found in the seemingly strange U.S. reaction to the crash of an American aircraft near Gander, Newfoundland, two weeks later. According to the Canadian Air Safety Board, it was ice on the wings that caused the downing of the chartered DC-8 on December 12. Officially, the ill-fated 248 American soldiers on board were heading home for Christmas. Nobody in the Pentagon hinted that some might have been secret operatives or that the charter company, Arrow Air, might have been doing more than routine transport work.

Our research suggests, however, that at least 20 of the crash victims were U.S. commandos returning from a counter-terrorism mission in the Middle East and that Arrow Air was no run-of-the-mill charter, but a CIA proprietary airline, and an important part of the contra supply network and the arms shuttle to Iran. In little-noticed Iran-contra testimony, one of Secord's associates admitted the company's involvement in both operations.

Given the airline's covert accounts, a prompt and thorough inquiry into the Gander crash might have thrust Iran-contra into the headlines a year before it surfaced. Even now the tragedy could come back to haunt Bush. As vice-president, he headed up Reagan's counter-terrorism task force and was responsible for monitoring operations of the sort allegedly undertaken by the commandos on the flight.

To imagine that he wasn't fully briefed on the circumstances surrounding their death, or the reported sensitivity of the carrier's mission, is unreasonable. According to long-time Army Criminal Investigation Department (CID) investigator Gene Wheaton, the tragedy was hushed-up because so much was at stake.

Even before the Gander crash faded from the headlines, another piece of the contra supply network suddenly came unhinged, and Bush again found himself handling repair work. The crisis arose in late 1985 when José Azcona Hoyo was elected to replace Suazo as President of Honduras. Lest the new regime renege on the deal the United States had levered out of its predecessor the previous spring, Bush was hustled to Tegucigalpa the following January for another round of "Let's Make a Deal."

In a recently released notebook, North keys the trip to a new "third country solicitation." He said the State Department wrote Bush's script, framing a good-cop/bad-cop scenario in which he was the pitchman while Admiral Poindexter muscled Azcona.

The script apparently played out as written. Within weeks Azcona approved a trial supply delivery to the contras, and the administration paid him with a security-assistance package worth $20 million.

With Bush again personally embroiled in contra support, his staff routinely got involved. In January 1986, Gregg's new deputy, Colonel Sam Watson, packed off to Honduras and El Salvador to survey supply bases and air fields. Inexplicably, Iran-contra investigators missed the significance of this trip. Only after a previously undisclosed Watson memo surfaced in a 1988 lawsuit did anyone realize that here was further proof the Vice President lied.

Written in February, shortly after Watson's return, the memo bears some scrawled notes from Gregg stating that "Rodriguez agrees with this." This belies *his* claim that he and his old friend never discussed the contras' supply problem before that August.

Equally damning are two other documents later generated by Gregg's staff. Both are "scheduling memos" written in anticipation of a May 1 meeting between Bush and Rodriguez, and both list "resupply of the contras" among topics to be discussed. When questioned about these documents, Rodriguez insisted that El Salvador, not the contras, was the only topic he'd broached with the Vice President. In later testimony before the Senate Foreign Relations Committee, Gregg cast the "resupply" notation as a reference to some sort of operation involving "resupply of the *copters*" which Rodriguez had been flying against Salvadoran rebels.

Possibly he and Rodriguez may have been telling the truth. But there is now plenty on record to indicate that by early 1986, Rodriguez's contra connection and indeed his increasingly troubled relationship with Secord were the talk of Bush's office.

Watson's own diaries, obtained during the Iran-contra hearings, reflect a preoccupation with such problems. One entry, dated July 29, recounts a White House staff meeting at which Rodriguez was accused of having "shut down pilots resupply." Three days later Watson noted a complaint from North that "F[elix] screwed up s[outhern] front," a reference to the contra operation in Costa Rica.

In his autobiography, Rodriguez admits that in his pique

over Secord's inefficiency and alleged money grubbing, he asserted control over the "private" supply shuttle. His main worry, apparently, was that Secord would commandeer the air fleet and sell it to the CIA for personal profit once congressional restrictions on contra aid eased. Always the crusader, Rodriguez wanted to ensure that the contras got their fair share.

Had the Iran-contra committees questioned Rodriguez about Watson's notebooks, they might have discovered that Bush's staff knew more earlier than anyone would admit. But again they pulled their punches, allowing both Rodriguez and Gregg to pretend that it was not until early August *after* the Congressional aid ban was loosened that Bush's men learned of the Rodriguez-Secord partnership.

If you believe Bush's official chronology, the revelation came on August 8, when Rodriguez sailed into Gregg's office to blow the whistle on Secord. Until then, supposedly, Gregg hadn't realized that Secord and North were running a private supply shuttle for the contras.

The notes Gregg took during this session do not read like a man caught by surprise. They plod through Rodriguez' revelations, as if they were no news, and contain a stunning phrase; "a swap of weapons for $ was arranged to get aid for the contras," that suggests insight beyond Rodriguez' problems with Secord.

Rodriguez told Iran-contra investigators that he couldn't remember mentioning a "swap" to Gregg. When Gregg was asked by a reporter if he might have been referring to the "diversion" of Iran arms profits to the contras, he countered that he'd known nothing about it.

Nobody on the investigating committees asked him whether the swap reference might relate to the aid-for-arms deals the administration had struck with Israel, Honduras, Guatemala and El Salvador. Nor was he pressed to explain why, after hearing Rodriguez out, he hadn't alerted Bush. His explanation, "It was a very murky business," left his congressional inquisitors nodding dumbly.

On October 5, a Sandinista gunner shot one of Secord's planes over Nicaragua, thus ending the contra supply operation. Appropriately, Rodriguez placed the first distress call to Watson, and soon Eugene Hasenfus, the lone surviving crew member, announced from jail in Managua that Rodriguez had honchoed the supply effort with Bush's knowledge.

Based on North's notebooks, the administration's reaction was to look for a scapegoat. On November 25, Poindexter apparently proposed that Bush contact the Israelis and persuade *them* to accept blame for the profits-diversion scheme. There is no evidence that Bush followed through. But the fact that Bush was the logical go-between lends weight to Brenneke's claim of collaboration between the Vice President and Jerusalem.

With Bush vulnerable to political damage from Contragate, he and his staff immediately launched a damage-control gambit. In mid-December, Gregg helped prepare the chronology that distanced Bush from the secret war. As time passed, Gregg increasingly mortgaged his own credibility to spare his boss. During the 1989 congressional hearings on his ambassadorial appointment to South Korea, Gregg dodged so many questions about Iran-contra that even a staunch Republican supporter confessed that some of his testimony "strain[s] belief."

As for Bush, he simply brazened it out, initially rebuffing questions, and finally seeking shelter behind the Iran-contra committees' concluding report, which didn't clear him but ignored him.

During the North trial last year, as the trade-off deals he'd negotiated with Honduras came to light, he continued to stonewall, declaring, "There was no quid pro quo." In the end Bush emerged without a scratch. Gregg got his ambassador post, and Brenneke just barely escaped jail.

For all of Bush's diligence in constructing a cover-up, however, he couldn't have done it without Congress' help. During the Iran-contra hearings, probers ignored certain leads to protect Israel and other allies. There is also evidence in North's notebook that some of them may have been guilty of collusion with the White House. The clue appears in a newly declassified entry written on March 4, 1985, just before Bush's first trip to Honduras.

On that date, according to North's shorthand, Robert McFarlane briefed four congressmen, including Henry Hyde and Bill McCollum, on the plan to seek "third country support" for the contras. A plan, as North described it, called for "center[ing] the activity in the White House."

Later, as members of the Iran-contra panels, Hyde and McCollum became the administration's most vocal cheerleaders, joining fellow Republicans in a minority report that got Bush off the hook.

Not only did the report find the Vice President ignorant of the supply effort, it dismissed the possibility "that any quid pro quo was sought or received in return for any third country contribution to the Resistance." In view of Hyde and McCollum's newly revealed inside knowledge, it's extraordinary that Bush still cites this as proof of his innocence.

Iran-contra prosecutor Lawrence Walsh once speculated that Irangate was really about the skewing of our constitutional checks and balances through imperial sleight-of-hand. It is one thing, he suggested, for a White House official to claim "executive privilege" when he doesn't want to tell Congress about a secret policy. That puts lawmakers on notice and triggers debate.

But if the White House tries to keep Congress out of the decision-making process by hiding the truth, he added, the scales are thrown out of kilter.

For all of its faults, the Iran-contra investigation left most Americans feeling that the scales had been unbalanced and that Reagan himself deserved much of the blame. But no one seemed to be able to fix Bush's responsibility because the heart of the scandal — the secret horse-trading on the contras' behalf — remained hidden.

With this last secret blown Bush now stands exposed, and

much more than we expected. He emerges not merely as Reagan's equal in subterfuge, but as his master in action, someone who actually helped execute a dirty-tricks scheme to hijack Congress' authority. Make no mistake. When Bush traveled to Central America in 1985 and 1986 to barter for contra support, he pursued a covert-action formula borrowed from his CIA days, the mobilizing of cutouts to protect the government. Only this time the object wasn't to keep some hostile foreign power in the dark, but all of us.[3]

The Bush-Reagan team rode to office on the issue of terrorism, pledging to halt it by never negotiating with terrorists and stopping others from doing so. For much of their Administration, federal law prohibited waging war on Nicaragua. Yet Bush attended dozens of meetings at which were discussed either our active role in the contra war or the secret supply of arms to Iran, which publicly he called a terrorist state.

Bush's assertion now that he didn't know of these activities is difficult to accept. An aide's notes record him being briefed on arms shipments to Iran as they were in progress. He says that he misunderstood; he thought that the sales were Israeli.

This doesn't add up. The records show that he had been told Israel was our front in the transactions. Bob Woodward reported, and Bush hasn't denied, that Bush was with Reagan when the President signed the Bible that was a gift to the ayatollah along with a planeload of missiles and arms. This remains an unsolved mystery.

Entering the picture at this point in 1984 was Dan Quayle. Yes, *the* Dan Quayle, at that time a relatively obscure senator from Indiana. Bush claims he picked Quayle as his 1988 running mate because of his strong right wing principles, no doubt true.

But he also owed Quayle a favor and, importantly, Quayle was someone Bush could trust.

---

3   Frank Snepp, "George Bush: Spymaster General," *Penthouse*, December 1990.

When the Administration expanded its illegal war against Nicaragua by secretly opening a southern front in Costa Rica, it used Quayle's office. Quayle's staff aide, Rob Owen, put North in touch with another Indianan, John Hull, who owned vast lands in northern Costa Rica.

Hull's property, containing six airstrips, became the secret contra arms depot and staging base. Owen went further as a facilitator. For his help Hull got a $375,000 U.S. government loan to build a lumber mill (he never built it), and Owen was trying to get him $500,000 more. Officials of the lending agency have testified that fraud was involved in that deal. We know how Qualye was rewarded.

Correspondence between Owen and North showed concern that drug-dealing among the contras could embarrass the operation, and even identified some drug dealers on the contra team. But no one followed through. Aircraft-maintenance receipts with signatures have been obtained which prove that the planes of a convicted Colombian cocaine cartel leader, George Morales, carrying contra leaders as well as drug smugglers were serviced and refueled at the Salvadoran base where Rodriguez managed the war supplies; Rodriguez reported to Bush, who supposedly ran the Administration's anti-drug program.

Contra arms were being supplied through Panama with the help of Manuel Noriega, but Bush says he didn't know this, which could put him in a class by himself among drug enforcers. In fact, when Bush took over the CIA in 1976, the agency had just received a high-level report from the Justice Department (the DeFeo report) citing Noriega's major role in drug trafficking; the report mentioned that U.S. drug agents had even proposed Noriega's assassination. Noriega was then working for the CIA.

The initial public reaction to the Iran-contra revelations inspired hope that after 40 years the nation would finally recognize that covert machinations overseas subvert our stated policy goals. But the hearings seem damage-controlled by the Administration, and the Democratic Party refused to follow it up, for reasons unknown.

As long as the out party ignores such duplicity in government, the United States has, in a sense, become a one-party state.[4]

The government allowed the Oliver North defense team to reveal evidence of Bush aiding the Nicaraguan contras in an agreement that keeps other sensitive information out of the courtroom, according to sources close to the negotiations.

The agreement disclosed Bush's role in promising millions of dollars in aid to Honduras, the contras' most important allies. But it concealed evidence that North's attorneys wanted to introduce that might have revealed covert military operations against Nicaragua by the CIA and foreign intelligence services, the sources said. These operations were referred to in the document only as "certain specified actions."

Bush refused to answer questions about this. "I am not going to comment on any aspect of the North trial while it's in progress," he said.

A member of the Tower Commission, which investigated the Iran-contra affair, acknowledged that the three-member commission never asked Bush about soliciting third-country aid.

"We knew we did not have the whole story," said former Sen. Edmund Muskie, D-Maine. The commission's other members were former Sen. John Tower, who lost a bitter confirmation battle to be Bush's defense secretary, and retired Gen. Brent Scowcroft, now Bush's national-security adviser.

Bush, who said that he was "out of the loop" when the Reagan Administration decided to sell arms to Iran, was a key backer of the initiative a White House memorandum acknowledged.

In 1986, shortly before the first U.S. weapons sale to Iran, then National Security Adviser John M. Poindexter wrote that while some top Administration officials opposed the transactions, *"most important, President and VP are solid in taking the*

---

4   Jonathan Kwitny, editorial in the *Los Angeles Times*, November 4, 1988.

position that we have to try."

The House and Senate panels that investigated the Iran-contra affair, described the memorandum, as "the first evidence [albeit hearsay] the committees have found concerning the Vice President's position on the Iran initiative."

Bush told reporters that if it "says that I stood with the President, the answer is yes, as I've been saying all along." He insisted that the disclosure would not damage his credibility.

Bush has said that he had missed key meetings involving the arms transactions, but repeated an earlier contention that "I expressed reservations" about the sales.

The congressional investigators and the commission headed by former Sen. Tower concluded that Bush's role in the Iran-contra affair was minor. The Senate's panel leaders, Chairman Daniel K. Inouye (D-Hawaii) and Vice Chairman Warren B. Rudman (R-N.H.) said in a joint statement that **nothing in the new evidence "would alter the committee's conclusions."**

But at least one other GOP leader, Alexander M. Haig, Jr., expressed displeasure with this.

Haig, who had previously denounced the Vice President's role in the Iran-contra scandal, said, "George Bush has a credibility crisis on this issue. The American people have a right to know just what he advised our President: to pay ransom or to not pay ransom?"

Throughout the 1988 presidential campaign, the Iran-contra affair put Bush in an uncomfortable position: If the Vice President did not know much about the sales, he was left out of decision-making in an administration where he has claimed an important role.

On the other hand, if Bush participated extensively this would raise questions about his judgment.

"I think he has not faced the issue directly; I think he will have to in the course of his [presidential] primary campaign.... The question becomes not one of intent but one of judgment," said Sen. William S. Cohen (R-Me.), a member of the Senate panel.

Bush told NBC's *Meet the Press,* "If I'd had a lot more knowledge of what was going on, I would have said, 'Don't do this.' Or if I had been sharp enough to see into the future, that a program that started out as not having arms for hostages turned into that, I'd have said, 'Don't do that.'"

So much for Iran-contra. Bush dodged that bullet. American voters apparently feared Willie Horton more than Manuel Noriega.

CHAPTER 8

The Bush-Whacking of Iraq

"I have opinions of my own, strong opinions, but I don't always agree with them."

President George Bush, leader of the free world

On July 25, 1990, eight days before the Iraqi invasion of Kuwait, U.S. Ambassador April Glaspie met with Iraqi leader Saddam Hussein at the Presidential Palace in Baghdad. The following is a transcript of their discussion:

Glaspie: I have direct instructions from President Bush to improve our relations with Iraq. We have considerable sympathy for your quest for higher oil prices, the immediate cause of your confrontation with Kuwait. As you know, I have lived here for years and admire your extraordinary efforts to rebuild your country. We know you need funds. We understand that, and our opinion is that you should have the opportunity to rebuild your country. We can see that you have deployed massive numbers of troops in the south. Normally that would be none of our business, but when this happens in the context of your other threats against Kuwait, then it would be reasonable for us to be concerned. For this reason, I have received an instruction to ask you, in the spirit of friendship not confrontation regarding your intentions: Why are your troops massed so very close to Kuwait's borders?

Hussein: As you know, for years now I have made every effort to reach a settlement on our dispute with Kuwait. There is to be a meeting in two days: I am prepared to give negotiations only this one more brief chance. When we [the Iraqis] meet [with the Kuwaitis] and we see there is hope, then nothing will happen. But if we are unable to find a solution, then it will be natural that Iraq will not accept death.

Glaspie: What solutions would be acceptable?

Hussein: If we could keep the whole of the Shatt al Arab, our strategic goal in our war with Iran, we will make concessions [to the Kuwaitis]. But, if we are forced to choose between keeping half of the Shatt and the whole of Iraq [i.e. including Kuwait], then we will give up all of the Shatt to defend our claims on Kuwait to keep the whole of Iraq in the shape we wish it to be. What is the United States' opinion on this?

Glaspie: (Pause, then she speaks very carefully) We have no opinion on your Arab-Arab conflicts, such as your dispute with Kuwait. Secretary [of State James] Baker has directed me to emphasize the instruction, first given to Iraq in the 1960s, that the Kuwait issue is not associated with America.

Saddam smiled.

On August 2, 1990, four days later, Saddam's massed troops invaded and occupied Kuwait.

On August 29, 1990, the *Miami Herald* reported that the State Department had been ordered to give its files concerning the July 25, 1990 meeting between Hussein and Glaspie to a federal judge to decide whether they must be released.

The Associated Press reported that the State Department was fighting a lawsuit filed by Public Citizens, which contended that the files must be released under the Freedom of Information Act.

U.S. District Judge Charles Richey, on August 28, stated that he needed to review the documents to determine whether the State Department properly withheld them from release. State contended that the documents were either "classified in the interest of national defense or foreign policy, or reflected the agency's deliberative process."

Richey wrote that Glaspie's public testimony may have "so thoroughly covered the subjects addressed in the withheld documents that the defendant may have waived the exemption."

The meeting in Baghdad between Glaspie and Hussein has been a critical issue in the debate over whether the United States led Hussein to believe it would not interfere if he invaded Kuwait, which he did a week later.

An Iraqi-released transcript of the meeting quoted Glaspie as saying that the United States would not take sides in "Arab-Arab" conflicts such as the border dispute with Kuwait.

However, Glaspie declared in Congressional testimony that she also told Hussein that the United States would insist that any dispute be settled peacefully.

On September 2, 1990, one month after Saddam's invasion of Kuwait, British journalists obtained a tape and transcript of the above Hussein-Glaspie meeting. Astounded, they confronted Ms. Glaspie.

Journalist 1: (Holding the transcripts up) Are the transcripts correct, Madam Ambassador? (Ambassador Glaspie did not respond).

Journalist 2: You knew Saddam was going to invade [Kuwait], but you didn't warn him not to. You didn't tell him America would defend Kuwait. You told him the opposite that America was not associated with Kuwait.

Journalist 1: You encouraged this aggression — his invasion. What were you thinking?

U.S. Ambassador Glaspie: Obviously, I didn't think, and nobody else did, that the Iraqis were going to take *all* of Kuwait.

Journalist 1: You thought he was just going to take *some* of it? But, how could you? Saddam told you that, if negotiations failed, he would give up his Iran [Shatt al Arab waterway] goal for the "*whole* of Iraq, in the shape we wish it to be." You *know* that includes Kuwait, which the Iraqis have always viewed as an historic part of their country!

(Ambassador Glaspie said nothing, pushing past the two journalists to leave.)

Journalist 1: America green-lighted the invasion. At a minimum, you admit signalling Saddam that some aggression was okay that the U.S. would not oppose a grab of the al-Rumeilah oil field, the disputed border strip and the gulf islands, territories claimed by Iraq?

(Again, Ambassador Glaspie said nothing as a limousine door slammed and the car drove off.)

The Bush Administration actively encouraged Hussein to pursue higher oil prices seven months before the invasion of Kuwait. According to high-level U.S. sources, it was discreetly suggested at a New York meeting in January that Iraq should engineer a big oil price rise in the Organization of Petroleum Exporting Countries (OPEC).

Transcripts leaked of discussions between U.S. and Hussein in the days around the invasion confirm the Bush Administration supported Saddam's oil price rise. The U.S. administration instigated a meeting between an American former ambassador, a member of the Council on Foreign Relations (CFR) still used by Bush on missions, and one of Saddam's top ministers to push this strategy.

The timing of this is significant. In January 1990, Saddam Hussein was a bankrupt dictator fighting for survival. Iraq, as a result of the long Iran-Iraq War and of Saddam's military spending, was broke.

Oil income of $12-13 billion couldn't cover basic needs. Civilian imports exceeded $11 billion in 1990; $3 billion of that for food. Military imports exceeded $7 billion and other foreign expenditures were estimated at about $1 billion. An extra $7 billion was needed to cover current expenditures. Iraq's foreign debt, about $1 billion in 1979, had risen to about $100 billion.

At the same time, Saddam had an army of 700,000 to demobilize with no jobs and a mutinous officer corps plotting against him. On January 6, a military coup nearly killed him. Politically, he was under siege. War-weary Iraqis expected, and had been promised, constitutional and democratic reforms. But in reality Saddam, who could not survive political liberalization, was tightening the screws on his regime. At the end of the year, he appointed his son and half brother to head the security forces.

Although eclipsed by events in Eastern Europe, demands for democratic reforms were beginning to shake the Middle East, including Gulf oil states. Kuwaitis were agitating for a return to their vigorous parliament of the 1970s. Yemen, the most populous country in the Gulf, was working on a democratic draft. Jordan was hesitantly liberalizing. The Palestinian intifada was smoldering on.

In these critical circumstances, the former American ambassador proposed an oil price increase to Saddam. In January 1990, the oil was $21 a barrel, but analysts expected that in the second quarter prices would fall to about $15 (as they did). Saddam could be in even deeper financial trouble by summer.

To meet the danger, Saddam was advised to commission a study on oil policy from the Washington Center for Strategic and International Studies, a foundation with links to Iraq.

Details have been kept secret, but it appears to advocate an aggressive oil policy for Arab producers.

Asked whether the U.S. presence in the Gulf should be reinforced to make up for force reduction in central Europe, Henry Schuler, the center's director, said that the internal stability of the governments in the region is his "main concern," but that the U.S. was powerless in that respect. Schuler felt that Arab oil producers could get $24 to $25 a barrel without consumers searching for alternative sources. Why leave money on the table for American consumers and the government? Criticizing those who did so could be a popular course, he observed.

This could be achieved by a change of policy in one or more of the key exporting Gulf states "one with the power to force all the states of the Gulf to follow suit," Schuler explained. The easiest way would be by "some change in leadership."

Both President George Bush and Secretary of State James Baker are oil men and the U.S. oil states Louisiana, Arizona, Alaska and even Texas were in financial trouble. The U.S. produces half the oil it consumes, so higher prices were an incentive for continued U.S. production.

In 1986, the U.S. had already acted to raise prices. The oil prices had collapsed to $8.90 and production declined. As vice-president, Bush traveled to Saudi Arabia to persuade King Fahd to pressure OPEC to raise prices. Fahd agreed. OPEC went back to its quota allowances and prices rose to $18. Saudi Oil Minister Sheikh Yamani, who had favored lower prices to obtain an increased market share for OPEC, was fired. Further, there was U.S. unease at becoming overly dependent on Middle East oil. An increase in oil prices was also a means of coping with security not just for Iraq, but in the Gulf generally, including Saudi Arabia.

The Bush Administration's deal with Saddam to raise oil prices can be tied down. First, it is significant that when Sadoun Hammadi, Iraq's Vice Prime Minister paraded Iraq's new views on oil prices around the Gulf states in early July, he demanded Schuler's $25 a barrel. This figure also reappears in two transcripts of U.S./Iraqi diplomatic exchanges leaked by Saddam to U.S. TV.

American neutrality must have encouraged Saddam, for in the previous months there had been warnings of his violent ambitions which had not elicited any U.S. response. In February, to raise oil prices, Saddam pursued anti-imperialist radical Arab nationalist rhetoric, historically the Arab sense of injustice at Israeli aggression towards Palestine and an oil price deemed unfair to Arabs.

In the fall of 1989, at a time when Iraq's invasion of Kuwait was nine months away and Saddam Hussein was desperate for money to buy arms, President Bush signed a Top-Secret National Security Decision Directive ordering closer ties with Baghdad and opening the way for $1 billion in aid, according to classified documents and interviews.

The $1 billion commitment, in the form of loan guarantees for the purchase of U.S. farm commodities, enabled Hussein to buy needed food on credit and to spend his scarce hard currency on the arms buildup that brought war to the Persian Gulf.

New aid from Washington was critical for Iraq in the last months of 1989 and early 1990 because international bankers had cut off all loans to Baghdad. They were alarmed that it was falling behind in repaying its debts but continuing to pour millions into arms purchases, even though the Iran-Iraq war had ended in 1988.

In addition to clearing the way for new financial aid, senior Bush aides, in the spring of 1990, overrode concern among other government officials and insisted that Hussein continue to be allowed to buy so-called "dual-use" technology — advanced equipment used for both civilian and military purposes. The Iraqis were given continued access to such equipment, despite evidence that they were working on nuclear arms and other weapons.

"Iraq is not to be singled out," National Security Council official Richard Haas declared at a high-level meeting in April 1990, according to participants' notes, when the Commerce Department proposed curbing Iraqi purchases of militarily sensitive technology.

Invoking Bush's authority, Robert Kimmitt, Undersecretary of State for Political Affairs, added, "The President doesn't want to single out Iraq."

Furthermore, the pressure in 1989 and 1990 to give Hussein crucial financial assistance and maintain his access to sophisticated U.S. technology were not isolated incidents. Rather, classified documents obtained by the *L.A. Times* reflected a long-secret pattern by Bush both as president and vice-president to support the Iraqi dictator. When objections arose, Bush and his aides suppressed the resistance.

The White House declined to comment.

As to the $1 billion in commodity loan guarantees, senior Bush aides armed with the presidential order NSD 26, insisted the credits be approved despite objections by three government agencies. These officials warned that aid violated American law, that the loans would not be repaid and that earlier assistance efforts were irregular.

Bush's involvement began in the early 1980s as part of the so-called "tilt" toward Iraq initiated by President Reagan to prop up Hussein in his war against Iran. Hussein's survival was seen as vital to U.S. efforts to contain the spread of Islamic fundamentalism and thwart Iran's bid for dominance in the Middle East.

Many in the American government, including Presidents Bush and Reagan, felt U.S. aid would push Hussein to moderate and help the Middle East peace process.

Classified records show that Bush's efforts on Hussein's behalf continued past the Iran-Iraq war and persisted despite widespread warnings from inside the American government that the policy was misdirected.

As it turned out, U.S. aid did not lead Hussein to become a force for peace. In the spring of 1990, as senior administration officials pushed for more financial aid, the Iraqi leader bragged that Iraq possessed chemical weapons and threatened to "burn half of Israel." Nor did he change his savage methods. In the summer of 1988, for example, he shocked the world by poisoning several thousand Kurds with gas.

Even today, the Iraqi nuclear and chemical weapons programs with the help of American technology haunt U.S. and United Nations officials as they root out elements that have survived the "allied victory" in the Persian Gulf War.

What drove George Bush to champion the Iraqis is not clear. It may have been single-minded pursuit of a policy after its original purpose had been accomplished and a failure to understand the nature of Hussein.

William B. Quandt, a Middle East expert at the Brookings Institution, told the *L.A. Times* in Feb. of 1992 that "when the Iran-Iraq War ended and Iran was really flat on its back, there should have been some immediate kind of repositioning of U.S. policy so you wouldn't give Saddam this signal that we were backing him as the big shot in the region. We missed so many cues. Saddam wasn't behaving as you might expect an exhausted, war weary leader to behave. He was showing that he had just won a war and he was a power to be reckoned with and he concluded that the Americans were not too upset about that."[1]

Much blame for failing to perceive Hussein's ambitions and building him up has fallen on mid-level officials and on the Commerce Department, which approved the sale to Iraq of $1.5 billion worth of American technology, as well as the Agriculture Department, which authorized $5 billion in loan guarantees.

However, classified documents from several agencies and interviews prove it was directives from the White House and State Department that guided relations with Iraq from the early 1980s through the Persian Gulf War and that Bush and officials played a prominent role in those initiatives.

For example:

- In 1987, Vice President Bush pressed the federal Export-Import Bank to provide hundreds of millions of dollars in aid for Iraq, the documents show, despite staff objections that the loans were not likely to be repaid as required by law.
- After Bush became president in 1989, documents show that senior officials in his administration lobbied the bank and the Agriculture Department to finance billions in Iraqi projects.
- As vice president in 1987, Bush met with Nizar Hamdoon, Iraq's ambassador to the United States, to assure him that Iraq could buy more dual-use technology. Three years later National Security Council officials blocked attempts by the Commerce Department and other agencies to restrict such imports.
- After Bush signed NSD 26 in October, 1989, Secretary of

---

1   Douglas Frantz & Murray Waas Bush, "Bush Secret Effort Helped Iraq Build Its War Machine," *Los Angeles Times*, February 23, 1992.

State James A. Baker III intervened with Agriculture
Secretary Clayton K. Yeutter to drop Agriculture's opposition to the $1 billion in food credits. Yeutter, now a
senior White House official, agreed and the first half of
the $1 billion was made available to Iraq back in 1990.

• As late as July 1990, one month before Iraqi troops stormed
into Kuwait City, officials at the National Security Council pushed the second installment of the $1 billion in loan
guarantees, despite the looming crisis in the region and
evidence that Iraq used the money for technology for its
nuclear weapons and ballistic-missile program.

An Agriculture Department official cautioned in February
1990 that, when all the facts were known about loan guarantees
to Iraq, the program could be another "HUD or savings and loan
scandal." Of the $5 billion given Iraq over an eight-year period,
American taxpayers have been stuck for $2 billion in defaulted
loans.

Washington's support of Iraq began in 1982. Hussein was in
the second year of his war with Iran and the conflict was not
going well for Baghdad. The Reagan administration, while
officially neutral, helped Iraq to contain the Ayatollah Khomeini.

U.S. relations with Iraq were severed in 1967 after the Arab-
Israeli War, but the biggest obstacle to renewed ties was the fact
that Iraq was on Washington's list of countries supporting international terrorism. That meant that most U.S. aid was prohibited
by law.

Yet, the State Department removed Iraq from the terrorism
list in February 1982, an action opposed by some within the
administration. Four former officials said there was no evidence
that Iraq's terrorism had waned.

"All the intelligence I saw indicated that the Iraqis continued to support terrorism to much the same degree as they had in
the past," said Noel Koch, then in charge of the Pentagon's
counter-terrorism program. "We took Iraq off the list and
shouldn't have.... We did it for political reasons."

This was supported by a secret 1988 memo in which Deputy Secretary of State John Whitehead wrote, "Even though it was removed from the terrorism list six years ago, [Iraq] had provided sanctuary to known terrorists, including Abul Abbas of Achille Lauro fame."

After Iraq was dropped from the list, Washington provided loan guarantees so it could buy rice and wheat through the Agriculture Department's Commodity Credit Corp.

Two years later in 1984, Bush pressed the federal Export-Import Bank to guarantee $500 million in loans so Iraq could build a controversial pipeline, according to classified government documents.

Throughout most of the Reagan administration, efforts were made to funnel arms as well as economic aid to Baghdad, sometimes through the Pentagon and sometimes through allies in the Middle East. Some plans failed to work, but government sources said that lots of arms reached Baghdad.

At one point in 1982, a trade of four American-made howitzers to Iraq for a Soviet T-72 tank was proposed, according to classified documents. The T-72 was important according to the Defense Intelligence Agency, because it was protected by a new type of armor, which might prove invulnerable to American firepower. A second plan in 1983 would have allowed Iraq to buy $45 million worth of 175-millimeter long-range guns and ammunition for a Soviet tank.

CHAPTER 9

BCCI Bush's Bank of Crooks, Criminals and Intelligence Agencies

As research for this book has shown, the dark shadow of George Bush has lurked in or about every important domestic or international event of the past thirty years.

The Bank of Commerce and Credit International scandal is no exception. Inevitably, Bush or some link to him would pop up unexpectedly in what could be the most widespread international banking scandal of the century.

For years, U.S. law enforcement officials knew that the BCCI was involved in money laundering and other illegal transactions.

Evidence has emerged that the Reagan-Bush and Bush-Quayle administrations:

- Funneled money to Saddam Hussein without congressional approval through BCCI;
- Maintained a commercial business venture with Gen. Noriega through BCCI;
- Cut off funding of the 1988 Dukakis presidential campaign by shutting down the Chicago BCCI branch.
- Blocked an investigation into drug money laundering through Robert Gates, a former U.S. Customs Commissioner, former CIA deputy director and now, Director of Central Intelligence.

While testifying before Senate investigators in his capacity as Customs Commissioner, Gates nicknamed BCCI "the bank of Crooks and Criminals."

BCCI was set up in the early 1970s by Arab and Asian financiers and staffed largely by Pakistani managers. So-called private banking, that is, departments of special financial services designed to avoid taxation and hide the assets of wealthy clients, was fast emerging as the most profitable business of the leading international megabanks, both on Wall Street and in England.

From the outset, BCCI was primarily a "private" bank, serving gulf oil magnates and other multimillionaire speculators who had something to conceal from authorities. BCCI's conspiratorial and far-flung financial network seemed custom-made for the CIA and the Mossad, Israel's secret service. They used BCCI to finance such major covert operations as the Afghan civil war, the secret arms deal with Iran, "black" subsidies to European political fronts via Switzerland, disinformation programs in Latin America, and the contra forces in Latin America.

Did shadowy Arab terrorists, such as the Abu Nidal group, also end up managing money through BCCI branches? "If they did, it was a set-up," said a veteran Customs investigator. "Any Arab militant who banked with BCCI was under CIA and Mossad surveillance and probably knew it. In Britain, the Mossad has become notorious for double operations during the 1980s, with agents of Middle Eastern descent who pretended to be 'Arab terrorists.' We need more evidence to know the score on this."

What U.S. law enforcement officials do know is that BCCI was used to finance murderous terrorist operations for the Mossad. As a textbook case, these knowledgeable sources cite Israeli arms and advice sold to the death squads of the Colombian cocaine cartel.

In 1990, the Justice Department sought to keep the Bank of Credit and Commerce International operating in Florida for undercover operations, according to congressional documents.

House Banking Committee Chairman Henry Gonzalez, D-Texas, said he found it "incredible" that the department would pressure Florida Comptroller Gerald Lewis "to keep open a crime-infested financial institution."

The attempt was unsuccessful. Lewis ordered BCCI to close its Florida operations in March 1990 and seized $15 million in assets after the institution admitted laundering drug money through its Tampa office.

The banking committee released copies of three letters, two written to Lewis by Charles Saphos, chief of the narcotic and dangerous drug section of the Justice Department's criminal division. The third letter was a Lewis response. In the first letter, dated Feb. 13, 1990, Saphos asked that BCCI's license be renewed in part because BCCI had agreed in a plea bargain to cooperate "in certain investigations."

Saphos wrote that the undercover investigations were part of an agreement reached with the bank when it pleaded guilty the previous month to about 30 charges. Lewis said that the bank's license to operate in Florida would expire on March 14, 1990, and added, "Because BCCI has pled guilty to felony charges, the ultimate decision of renewal becomes a difficult one." Lewis requested a meeting with Saphos to learn more about the department's request.

Saphos replied that he was not requesting Florida to renew the bank's license. He told Lewis that under the plea bargain agreement, BCCI might be asked to open or continue accounts for people who were under investigation by the Justice Department.

The President was seething. Gates, his nominee to be Director of the CIA, was caught up in an old scandal, and the Senate Intelligence Committee put his confirmation hearings on hold.

Standing outside his vacation home in Kennebunkport, Bush wagged his finger at reporters and railed against politicians, "They ought not to accept a rumor. They ought not to panic and run like a covey of quail because somebody has made an allegation against a man whose word I trust," Bush said, his voice rising. *"What have we come to in this country where a man has to prove his innocence against some fluid, movable charge?.... I just don't think it's the American way to bring a good man down by rumor and insinuation."*

It may not be the American way, but in Washington, press exposure is often the beginning of the end for high-profile presidential appointees.

Gates has been done in once before. In 1987, when he was deputy director of the CIA, Gates was forced to withdraw his nomination to be chief because of unanswered questions about his role in the Iran-contra scandal.

For the next four years he rehabilitated himself, cultivating Congress and the press from his deputy post at the CIA and then as George Bush's deputy national-security adviser.

Iran-contra faded off the front pages. So when Gates was again nominated in May to replace retiring CIA chief William Webster, the White House hoped the scandal was finally behind him. They guessed wrong.

The lengthy investigation by independent counsel Lawrence Walsh finally produced a breakthrough. Former CIA official Alan Fiers, who once ran the agency's Central American Task Force, admitted that he and, other senior CIA officials had known of the diversion of funds to the contras and that they had withheld this from Congress. Members of the Senate Intelligence Committee were angry that they had been misled by the agency they are supposed to oversee.

It is not certain whether Gates was among the deceivers. But the Senate delayed confirmation hearings to gather more information, leaving Gates to twist as damaging press stories started. ABC's *Nightline* charged that the CIA failed to tell Congress about a covert operation, which the report claimed Gates supervised, that funneled arms to Iraq in the mid-80s. At the time the U.S. was backing Iraq against Iran by providing intelligence information and, according to the *Nightline/Financial Times*, cluster bombs and fuel-air explosives.

The White House issued a denial, and Senate investigators said they saw no evidence to back up the report. Nonetheless, committee sources told *Newsweek* that the Gates nomination "is in deep trouble." As one aide put it, "We're back to where we were with him in 1987."

Beyond Gates, Fier's revelations embarrassed Webster and the Agency. Webster had assured David Boren, chairman of the Senate Intelligence Committee, that the late William Casey was the only CIA official who knew of the illegal diversion. "What Fiers is saying is that the committee was systematically lied to and people in the agency took part in the cover-up," said another committee source.

Fiers agreed to plead guilty to two misdemeanor counts of withholding information from Congress. In late summer 1986, Fiers says, Oliver North told him the United States was selling arms to Iran and using the proceeds to aid the contras. Fiers says he told the head of the Agency's Latin American division, who ordered him to report it to Clair George, deputy director for operations.

George served directly under Gates. "Now you are one of a handful of people who knows," George told Fiers, according to Fiers. Both Fiers and George later told Congress they knew nothing of the diversion until Attorney General Edwin Meese III made it public on Nov. 25, 1986.

The intelligence committee has no evidence that Fiers or George told Gates of the diversion. Gates has said that Casey cut him out of the loop on the Latin American operations and that he didn't pry.

He admits he picked up some hints of the diversion before it became public, but says he ignored them because he considered the evidence "flimsy."

That was the accepted explanation until Fiers revealed that Casey wasn't the only one at the CIA aware of the diversion. "Now you have a situation where the man above Gates and the men below him knew what was going on," says Sen. Howard Metzenbaum (D-Ohio). "You have to wonder how come he didn't know."

Former U.S. Customs Commissioner William von Raab and at least one other senior law enforcement investigator reportedly told investigators that in 1988, while serving as deputy director, Gates obstructed an investigation into drug-money laundering at BCCI. The CIA is known to have used BCCI's global network to funnel funds to the Mossad, not just from its own "black" accounts, but from oil-rich Arab states, who wanted to leave no paper trail or public record of payoffs.

Under pressure from Bush, Gates eventually withdrew his nomination a second time hoping to curtail further revelations about Bush-BCCI connections.

Some of the millions obtained by the Israeli secret service from Saudi slush funds and other gulf sources were laundered through BCCI and moved to CenTrust Bank, Miami's largest and most freewheeling savings and loan center, sources revealed.

CenTrust, seized by federal regulators, was headed by David Paul, a billionaire speculator now under criminal investigation for alleged financial irregularities.

The secret funds transferred to CenTrust via BCCI went to the Mossad which drew on them in early 1987 to finance its covert stations in Latin America, including Panama and Colombia.

There the drug deals and death squads run by Israeli agents undermined the Bush Administration's narcotics strategy, and led to the assassination of numerous Colombian officials, clashing with the efforts of U.S. law enforcement teams in the region.

According to Chicago journalist Sherman Skolnick, from secret court documents he has uncovered, Bush and Saddam split $250 billion worth of Persian Gulf oil kickbacks, which were funneled through the scandal-ridden Bank of Credit and Commerce International (BCCI).

"These are not government-to-government transactions. These are private transactions between Bush as an individual and Saddam as an individual — transactions amounting to billions of dollars. The House Banking Committee under chairman, Rep. Henry Gonzalez (D-Texas), has already stated that BCCI worked with Banca Nazionale del Lavoro (BNL). BNL is the largest bank in Italy. It has five branches in the United States. The Bush-

Saddam transactions went through these two banks."

Skolnick reported that he attended a hearing involving federal litigation that touches directly on the BCCI scandal and which included documents that implicate Bush and Saddam in private business deals.

The case in question is case No. 90 C 6863, *The People of the State of Illinois ex rel Willis C. Harris vs the Board of Governors of the Federal Reserve System*, in the U.S. Court of Appeals for the Seventh Circuit in Chicago.

According to Skolnick:

> The case involves records of BNL's [Banco Nazionale del Lavoro, the largest bank in Italy] Chicago unit which the House Banking Committee is trying to get and which were also in the possession of the Federal Reserve Board.
>
> The records demonstrate private transactions involving $250 billion in oil money kickbacks from the entire gulf region paid to Saddam Hussein. The Federal Reserve Board wanted Congressman Gonzalez to agree to never use these records in any of his congressional reports. He was only to be allowed to look at the records. But the congressman refused to sign the secrecy oath that the Fed demanded.
>
> Following the May 10 hearing I told the attorneys that I had heard what the records were about. I spelled out these huge private transactions between Bush and Saddam. The attorneys said, "Mr. Skolnick, you are absolutely correct."
>
> The attorneys said that because Congressman Gonzalez would not sign the secrecy oath that the truth would come out regarding the secret arrangements involving those deals [between Bush and Saddam].
>
> One of the lawyers said, "Well, that's true. I want you to know that what is involved here are non-bank records that the Justice Department [doesn't want released]."
>
> "Non-bank records" is a euphemism for bank records that a bank doesn't want released. This involves monumental amounts of a joint business deal between Bush and Saddam that they don't want released. For 10 years Saddam Hussein was the bully of the Persian Gulf. The OPEC oil producers in

the gulf had to kick back 25 percent of the amount from the Western oil companies to Saddam, and the money went through the bank. There was upwards of a trillion dollars' worth of oil from the gulf shipped (from 1980 to 1990) to the West. From these oil deals, Saddam got kickbacks to the tune of $250 billion arranged by George Bush and oil companies such as Pennzoil which are connected to Bush [one of the heads of Pennzoil].

Saddam split these kickbacks from the oil companies with George Bush and others. The Chicago case in question [mentioned above] came up before a three-judge appeals panel. We found out that one of the judge's law clerks leaked out information that one of the judges is pressing to release the records. The release of these records would put George Bush in jail, just like that.

The Justice Department then started circulating stories that one of the panel members is being investigated for eight instances of bribery in other cases. We know about these other cases. However, the Justice Department only wants this information about the bribery cases known in order to blackmail the three-judge panel not to release the documents relating to Bush and Saddam.

Skolnick revealed that his investigation pinpointed efforts within even the House Banking Committee itself to sabotage Gonzalez's investigation of the Bush-Saddam-BCCI scandal. According to Skolnick:

> One of my contacts spoke to Mr. Gonzalez, and it appears that the Congressman and his secretary are aware of these saboteurs. They are being sabotaged.
>
> On the Senate side the investigation is also being hampered. On June 13 the *Wall Street Journal* pointed out that Sen. [John] Kerry [D.-Mass.] who is investigating BCCI became chairman of the Democratic Senate Campaign Committee which received large contributions from BCCI. There's something outrageous going on here.
>
> There is the third investigation being conducted by Man-

hattan District Attorney Morgenthau. The key records impli-
cating Bush's deals with Saddam and Noriega are in the
hands of the Bank of England, which is seizing all of these
BCCI branches, as outlined earlier.

Now here's the way it could be explained. On the one
hand they are either trying to cover up for Bush or else they
want these records to blackmail the Bush White House. Pick
whichever explanation you're comfortable with. I don't know
whether there will be an honest government investigation
since the one honest investigation being conducted by Mr.
Gonzalez is being sabotaged by people on his committee.

It's worth noting, incidentally, that the money paid to the
Iranians in the so-called October Surprise and Iran-contra
scandals went through BCCI and BNL. That's why the whole
thing is a runaway scandal. This case involves what amounts
to the largest tax-evasion case in history, and George Bush
most likely would have to go prison.

In an interview with Tom Valentine of Radio Free America,
Skolnick continued:

The bulk of the money went through BCCI. That bank
was formed in the 1970s with seed money from the Bank of
America, the largest shareholders of which are the Rothschilds
of Chicago, Paris, London and Switzerland.... The bank is
also linked to the financial affairs of former President Jimmy
Carter and his friend and one-time budget director, banker
Bert Lance.

Some of the details about the Democrats who have been
involved in this whole affair have been published, for example, in the May 3 issue of the *Wall Street Journal*. During
the 1988 presidential campaign, additionally, BCCI was one
of the major financiers of the Michael Dukakis campaign.

On the Columbus Day weekend in 1988 at the behest of
the Reagan White House, BCCI's facilities in the United
States were seized, including their branch in Chicago. It was
claimed that BCCI was in the drug-money laundering
business...BCCI operate[d] in 73 countries and had 400
branches. BCCI financed the Democratic Party in the United

States and arranged deals for Republicans outside the United States.

There were two purposes behind the seizure of the BCCI Chicago branch:

One, to stop BCCI's funding of the Dukakis campaign so that Dukakis would have no money for television advertisements in the remaining weeks of the 1988 campaign.

Two, to impound and suppress records at the Chicago branch regarding kickbacks to Saddam which tend to incriminate George Bush in his joint business ventures with the Iraqi dictator.

I point out one other thing: The same bank has records showing joint business ventures between Gen. Manuel Noriega, former dictator of Panama, and George Bush. In January of 1990, the federal prosecutor in Tampa had former top officials of Florida's branch on trial. They were allowed to escape prison with only a slap on the wrist and a small penalty. Here's why: They told the Justice Department that if they were going to go to prison, they had documents from their bank showing that George Bush had private business ventures through their bank with a series of dictators including not only Saddam and Noriega but others as well.

What's interesting is that the records of the Florida branch of BCCI were not seized, but the Chicago branch records were seized. The reason for this is that the bulk of the $10 billion in kickbacks to Saddam went through the Chicago branch. This is almost certainly the same reason that the Justice Department is not interested in bringing charges against the Chicago bankers. They can use the same threat against Bush that the Florida bankers have made.

The Justice Department not only seized the Chicago branch records to damage the Dukakis campaign, but to cover up the joint business ventures between Bush and various dictators, as I've mentioned. Another bank, the Banco Nazionale del Lavoro [BNL] is also involved in these deals. Their Chicago subsidiary also had records relating to these deals.

Rep. Gonzalez, chairman of the House Banking Committee, was in the process of seizing these records via a congressional subpoena. However, on December 28, 1990, a federal judge in Chicago, Brian Duff, who has connections with the Federal Reserve, impounded those records and chased Gonzalez's attorney out of court and called him names, saying he was acting like "an 800-pound gorilla." The judge ordered Gonzalez not to use any of the records that he already has and ordered him to give the other documents back....

Saddam's oil was shipped to Texaco. In 1985 a Texas jury, at the behest of Pennzoil, issued the largest damage verdict in American history against Texaco. Pennzoil claimed that Texaco damaged them in a deal with Getty Oil. Who owns Pennzoil? George Bush and his friends.

Some of this came out in an obituary in the *Chicago Tribune*. It referred to "George Bush and his partner, William Liedtke Jr. and Liedtke's brother." It said that "In the mid-1950s [the Liedtke brothers] teamed up with then-oilman George Bush and John Overby to form Zapata Oil Co. Then they went on to form Pennzoil."

Texaco appealed to the Texas Supreme Court, which upheld the verdict but refused to review it. Thereafter there were stories in the press in various parts of the country that judges on the Texas Supreme Court are "corrupt." Texaco went to the U.S. Supreme Court because they were told that they had to put up a $12 billion "appeals bond." (It would have been the largest appeals bond in the history of the world).

Bush leaned on the Supreme Court — let's say it like it is — Bush corrupted the Supreme Court to grant no remedy to Texaco. Believe me, legal scholars were scratching their heads, but there's no doubt about what happened. As a result of this Texaco fell under the domination and supervision of Pennzoil.

Where did the kickbacks to Saddam reportedly come from? They came from the deals between Texaco and its subsidiaries purchasing oil from Iraq. There's where the $200 billion comes from, and 5 percent of that is $10 billion. There's no way in the world that Bush would not have known about those kickbacks, which he obviously supervised. As far as the kickbacks, there has been something published about them. The November 29, 1989 issue of the *Wall Street Journal* reported that IRS officials say that officials of the BNL got $290,000 in kickbacks from Saddam in his deals.

The nature of these "deals" are left out of the article. Obviously, some of these deals are the ones in which Bush was involved. As I perceive it, there has been falsification of records and obstruction of justice. By what right does the White House lean on the Supreme Court to damage Texaco for the benefit of George Bush and his Pennzoil company?

In the last couple of weeks the press is trying to put all of the blame for the Noriega deals and for the Saddam deals on Clark Clifford. I've interviewed several sources who know Clifford and his wife. His wife is going around crying to friends that her husband is about to be indicted and framed by the White House to protect Bush himself from going to prison. I don't know if Clark Clifford is an angel or not, but I do know it's wrong to blame all this on Clifford and ride him into jail without Bush going along behind him. They are trying to make it look like the BCCI scandal is a Democratic Party albatross and focus everything on Clifford. I don't say any of this lightly. I'm saying there is a reasonable basis for grand juries to indict George Bush.

As far as I'm concerned, there's only one independent source in this country, and those are grand jurors.... I've also talked to several sources close to Gonzalez [and they said] that he is considering going before Congress and demanding that the Justice Department prosecute Bush on these kickbacks to Saddam that went through BCCI and BNL, which Bush knew about and which his financial interests in those oil companies arranged.

Gonzalez's closest friends say that the only thing prevent the congressman from going on the floor of the House and urging Bush's prosecution is that the White House is invoking some sort of "national security" matter involving these two banks.

Dark shadows keep emerging from George Bush's past. Yet somehow — as if by magic — he scrapes through unscathed.

Who said Ronald Reagan was the teflon President?

CHAPTER 10

The Sins of the Fathers...and the Sons...and the Brothers

This "...contrasts with Bush's twitching, flailing body language and ghastly, pained grin, which betray incredible anxiety."

John Taylor, *New York Magazine*, 1992

In the cozy, back-scratching, name-dropping world of the Bush family, it is whom you know that makes all the difference. Having the same last name as the most powerful man in the western world is the same as buying an inexpensive ticket to enter a can't-miss world of lucrative business deals.

It's a world of preferential treatment where public officials condone the type of conduct that would be prosecuted if the name were not Bush. This has long been a historical pattern for the Bush family, who have made a dubious tradition out of using politics and CIA manipulations to foster their various business enterprises.

Members of the Bush family have repeatedly displayed their adeptness at finding ways to capitalize on the fact they are related to the President. They have also been skillful at avoiding any responsibility and ducking any punishment for highly questionable misdeeds, so it must have been something of a shock for Jonathan J. Bush to be actually caught for doing something wrong. Of course, the price that Jonathan J. Bush paid turned out to be typically light for a Bush — not much more than a slap on the wrist.

Jonathan is the brother of President Bush and head of J. Bush & Co., a New York brokerage house. He was fined $30,000 for trading stocks for about 800 accounts in Massachusetts without registering in the state as a broker, officials said on July 26.

Bush agreed to pay the fine and limit the company's business in Massachusetts for one year, according to Neil Sullivan, securities division chief for the Massachusetts Secretary of State.

J. Bush & Co. signed a consent decree that includes an offer to buy back an undetermined number of shares it had sold to Massachusetts customers since January 1988, Sullivan said, adding, "What we're really saying here is that the state doesn't have confidence that Mr. Bush has adequate compliance procedures in place to protect smaller investors." The company is now registered in Massachusetts.

In January 1991, Harken Energy Corp. of Grand Prairie, Texas, signed an oil-production sharing agreement with the government of Bahrain, a tiny island off the east coast of Saudi Arabia. The deal gives Harken the exclusive exploration, development production, transportation and marketing rights to most of Bahrain's offshore oil and gas reserves. The territories covered by the pact lie sandwiched between the world's largest oil field, off the shore of Saudi Arabia, and one of the biggest natural gas fields off the shore of Qatar.

At the time the deal was announced, oil industry analysts marveled at how this unknown company, with no previous international drilling experience, had landed such a valuable concession. "This is an incredible deal, unbelievable for this small company," Charles Strain, an energy analyst at Houston's Lovett Underwood Neuhaus & Webb, told *Forbes Magazine*. Not mentioned in the article was that George W. Bush, eldest son of the President, sits on Harken's board and is a $50,000-a-year "consultant" to the chief executive officer. Bush also holds roughly $400,000 in Harken stock.

The President's son would not be the only notable figure to profit if Harken struck oil in Bahrain. Involved also are: the billionaire Bass family of Fort Worth, which will pay for Harken's Bahrain expedition for a cut of the profits; Harvard University, which, through an affiliate, is Harken's largest shareholder; South African tobacco, liquor and natural resources magnate, Anton Rupert, a major Harken stockholder; and wealthy Saudi Arabian businessman, Abdullah Taha Bakhsh, who also holds a large stake in the company.

It is not just these wealthy and powerful groups that make Harken noteworthy, however. Research by the *Observer* reveals that Harken has links to institutions involved in drug smuggling, foreign currency manipulation and the CIA's role in the destabilization of the Australian government.

While it should be stressed that none of the players involved in Harken stands accused of any improper or illegal activity, the company's association with these institutions raises serious questions. Many of these connections are subtle, hidden behind layers of corporate stealth. To fully appreciate Harken and its milieu, however, these connections must be fully examined.

George W. Bush's involvement in Harken was revealed in Oct. 1990 by *Houston Post* investigative reporter Pete Brewton. At the time, Brewton questioned young Bush about Harken's deal with Bahrain, which was then threatened by hostilities in the Persian Gulf. Moreover, as the *Village Voice* reported in January, "Harken's investments in the area will be protected by a 1990 agreement Bahrain signed with the U.S. allowing American and 'multi-national' forces to set up permanent bases in that country." Bush, who is the managing general partner of the Texas Rangers baseball club, told the *Post* it would be "inappropriate to say the U.S. armed forces in the Persian Gulf are protecting Harken's drilling rights off Saudi Arabia."

"I don't think there is a connection," Bush said. "I don't feel American troops in Saudi Arabia are preserving George Bush, Jr.'s drilling prospects. I think that's a little far-fetched."

In his interview with the *Post*, Bush mentioned that he had sold a large portion of his Harken stock "in June or July" 1990, weeks before Iraq's invasion of Kuwait on August 2. Within days of the invasion, the value of Harken shares dropped dramatically. Brewton could find no record of the transaction on file with the Security and Exchange Commission (SEC).

The mystery of the missing documents was resolved last April 4, when the *Wall Street Journal* reported that Bush failed to report the "insider" stock sale until March, nearly eight months after the deadline for disclosing such transactions. According to the *Journal*, documents filed with the SEC indicate that on June 22, 1990, Bush sold 212,140 shares of his Harken stock for $4 per share. The sale, representing 66 percent of Bush's holdings in the company, raised $848,560.

Bush sold his Harken shares at near top market value. One week after Iraqi troops marched into Kuwait, for example, Harken traded for just $3.03 per share, down nearly 25 percent from the price Bush received for his shares seven weeks earlier. In the past year, Harken has never closed higher than $4.62 per share and as low as $1.12. Since the war ended in February, Harken has rebounded and is once again trading at around $4 per share.

Under SEC regulations, Bush should have reported the sale by July 10, 1990. The *Journal*, however, said Bush did not disclose it until March, 1991. In the past, the SEC has mounted civil suits against flagrant violators of insider-trading rules, but such actions are rare.

Bush described himself to the *Post* as a "small, insignificant" stockholder. According to the company's 1989 proxy statement, Bush owned 345,426 shares of Harken's common stock, or less than 1.1 percent of the total.

News reports in 1989, however, identified Bush as the second-largest non-institutional stockholder. The company's 1990 proxy statement indicates Bush owns 105,000 shares of common stock, less than 1 percent of the outstanding total, and has warrants to purchase another 28,286 at a substantially reduced price.

As a director of Harken, Bush earned at least $20,000 last year, according to the company's proxy statement. He received an additional $120,000 as a "consultant" to Harken President and CEO Mikel D. Faulkner. This year, Bush will receive $50,000 for his consulting services in addition to his pay as a director.

Following the collapse of world oil prices in 1986, Bush merged his Midland oil company, Spectrum 7 Exploration, with Harken. According to the *New Republic*, Bush "got no cash or role in Harken's management, but he did get 1.5 million shares of Harken restricted stock, warrants to buy 200,000 more, and a seat on Harken's board." At the time of the merger, Harken had annual revenues of just $4.4 million. In 1990, the company took in over $822 million. Despite this rapid growth, however, Harken has not made money since the merger. In 1990, the company lost over $8.3 million.

As a result of its deal with Bahrain, however, Harken's fortunes could change. Although the only other oil-exploration effort off the shore of Bahrain came up dry in 1961, Harken officials believe the area holds vast potential.

In 1989, Bahrain's one producing onshore oil field yielded 42,000 barrels a day. The country's estimated underground reserves for 1990 totaled 112 million barrels out of the 660-billion barrels in the entire Persian Gulf region. "It's a wildcat prospect, so you have to give it a low probability of success," Faulkner told the Fort Worth *Star-Telegram*, "but it's the kind of thing that, if it hits, could make a ten-fold increase in the value of the company."

Under the agreement with Bahrain, Harken will drill up to six exploratory wells over a three-year period. If Harken finds oil, it would share the production revenues with the government of Bahrain for the next 35 years. Neither Harken nor the Bahraini government will disclose how those revenues would be divided.

Harken estimates the cost of drilling the first well will run between $12 million and $13 million. Analysts say the cost of drilling six wells could go as high as $50 million. For cash-strapped Harken, these costs presented a formidable obstacle. Once the deal with Bahrain was signed, therefore, Harken began looking for deep-pocketed partners to fund the project.

At least 30 eligible suitors soon came forward, including five major oil companies. Harken eventually settled on Bass Enterprises Production Co., the oil and gas exploration and development arm of Fort Worth's billionaire Bass family. Bass Enterprises is headed by Sid and Lee Bass, sons of oil tycoon Perry Richardson Bass.

In July 1990, Harken announced that Bass Enterprises would finance the first three exploratory wells in Bahrain. After drilling the three initial wells, Bass could withdraw from the project, but would forfeit any revenues from oil production. If Bass funds an additional three wells, however, it would earn a 50-percent share of the profits Harken receives from its agreement with Bahrain. Current plans call for drilling to begin in the fall of 1992.

George W. Bush and the Bass brothers are not the only children of prominent parents involved in Harken. Harken director and former chairman Alan G. Quasha is the son of powerful Philippines lawyer William H. Quasha. Published accounts have documented connections between the senior Quasha and Australia's infamous Nugan-Hand bank.

Official Australian government investigations during the late 1970s and early 1980s revealed Nugan-Hand's involvement in drug money laundering and ties to the U.S. military and intelligence community.

Nugan-Hand co-owner and vice-chairman, Michael Jon Hand, a Green Beret war hero and CIA operative, was also a "pal of dope-dealers and of retired and not-so-retired military intelligence officials," according to *The Crimes of Patriots*, by former *Wall Street Journal* reporter Jonathan Kwitny.

In 1977, the Australian Narcotics Bureau released a report detailing Nugan-Hand's involvement in a drug smuggling network that "exported some $3 billion [Australian] worth of heroin from Bangkok prior to June 1976," according to Australia's *Sunday Pictorial*. Moreover, according to a 1984 article in *Mother Jones*, former CIA officers and Iran-contra figures Theodore Shackley and Thomas Clines, along with their subordinate Edwin Wilson (who is currently imprisoned for selling plastic explosives to Libya) used Nugan-Hand funds for a variety of covert operations, including the destabilization of the Australian government in 1975.

In April 1980, as Australian government investigators closed in on Nugan-Hand, the co-administrators of the bank's Manila offices, U.S. Gen. LeRoy J. Manor and British subject Wilfred Gregory, turned to their lawyer, William Quasha, for advice, according to Kwitny.

In addition to his duties with Nugan-Hand, Manor was chief of staff for the U.S. Pacific Command and the U.S. government liaison with Philippine President Ferdinand Marcos.

Gregory was Nugan-Hand's original representative in the Philippines and a friend of Marcos' brother-in-law, Rudwig Rocka, whose family deposited $3.5 million in the bank, according to Kwitny.

Gregory has stated that Manor's decision to flee the Philippines to avoid punishment was inspired by a conversation with William Quasha. According to Kwitny, "Gregory says William Quasha 'arranged for Manor to leave the country. He told me to go, too.' He said, 'You could wind up in jail.' The three-star general, according to Gregory, left overnight."

In an interview with Kwitny, Quasha said that attorney-client privilege prevented him from divulging whether he told Manor and Gregory they faced possible imprisonment, or whether he advised Manor to leave the Philippines. "I'm not confirming or denying that I gave General Manor such advice," Quasha said.

Harken's familial ties to Nugan-Hand and, indirectly, the intelligence community, are reminiscent of another of the company's father-son relationship, that of George W. Bush and his father.

Harken, the Quashas and other key Harken figures have additional ties to Nugan-Hand through dealings with a Swiss bank. William Quasha's son Alan, the Harken director, is an attorney with the New York law firm of Quasha, Wessley & Schneider. He is also a director of North American Resources Limited (NAR), one of the principal stockholders in Harken.

According to Harken's proxy statement, NAR, which owns 20.24 percent of Harken's stock, is a partnership between Quasha's family and the Richemont Group Limited, a publicly-traded Swiss company.

The Richemont Group is controlled by South-African billionaire Anthony E. "Anton" Rupert. NAR is also the parent company of Intercontinental Mining and Resources Limited (IMR), another major Harken shareholder, according to Harken's proxy statement. The proxy also states that IMR "and its affiliates" are major shareholders in two Harken subsidiaries, E-Z Serve Corp. and Texas Power Corp. In 1989, E-Z Serve sold 80 percent of its Hawaiian subsidiary, Aloha Petroleum, Ltd., to IMR for $12 million. IMR later sold its interest in Aloha.

Alan Quasha also sits on the board of Frontier Oil and Refining Co. of Denver, along with Harken President Mikel Faulkner. Like the Richemont Group, Frontier is headed by Anton Rupert. Last October, Harken and Frontier announced that E-Z Serve would purchase Frontier Oil Corp., a subsidiary of Frontier Oil and Refining. The Frontier group later backed out of the deal.

Harken is clearly not a typical small oil company. Its allure to some of the world's richest and most powerful men, and ability to secure potentially valuable concessions, perplex even veteran industry analysts. The company's complex web of financial and family relationships is considered extraordinary.

Meanwhile, a company that employs President Bush's brother Prescott as a consultant, stands to benefit if the President clears the way for the shipment of two satellites to China by the Hughes Aircraft Co. U.S. officials and foreign diplomats have said President Bush was expected to approve exporting the satellites. The action would represent one of the measures the Administration is taking to improve strained relations with China.

Asset Management International Financing & Settlement, Ltd., a New York firm for which Prescott Bush is a consultant, has a contract to provide communications connecting more than 2,000 professional and university offices in China.

Company executives said that the Hughes satellites would be "advantageous" for its project, which is a 50-50 joint venture with the Chinese government. In addition, Asset Management's executive vice president said in an interview that the company could obtain more communications business in China if the satellites are launched.

Prescott Bush, an international businessman with extensive business contacts in Asia, has denied using his younger brother's position to help him, and there is no substantial indication that the President's foreign policy has been affected by his brother's business dealings.

White House Press Secretary Marlin Fitzwater said both the President and his brother were not aware of any direct relationship between Asset Management's business activities and Hughes Aircraft, which is supplying the satellites.

"I talked to the President, and he said he is unaware of any relationship or any activity involving Hughes Aircraft," Fitzwater said. "Then I called Prescott, and he also was unaware of any association involving Hughes Aircraft."

A U.S. diplomat, describing Prescott Bush's dealings in China, said in an interview, "He was smart enough not to mention his brother's name, and the Chinese were smart enough to make the connection."

President Bush, who headed the U.S. mission in China in the mid-1970s, sent National Security Adviser Brent Scowcroft and Deputy Secretary of State Lawrence S. Eagleburger to Beijing, to prevent China from drifting into isolation as a result of international outrage over the June 3-4 massacre of pro-democracy demonstrators.

The overture brought criticism on Capitol Hill, where Democrats accused the President of moving too swiftly without concessions from the Chinese. Last June, in response to congressional pressure, Bush imposed sanctions against China, including a ban on the sale or export of equipment with possible military uses. Last fall, Congress enacted a provision that specifically banned the export of satellites to China unless the President granted a waiver "in the national interest."

Scowcroft's trip to Beijing was the latest and most dramatic step by the Administration to ease the impact of the restrictions. If Bush approves exporting the Hughes satellites to China, it could heighten the controversy in Congress.

Los Angeles-based Hughes Aircraft has been seeking final approval from the White House to sell two of its communications satellites, one to an Australian state-owned company called Ausat and the other to a Hong Kong consortium called Asiasat. Both satellites would be launched on Chinese rockets in China's Sichuan province. The satellites are designed to provide vital communication links across Asia and Australia and would be a boon to the joint venture between the Chinese government and Asset Management, an international financial-services company.

Company records list Prescott Bush as a member of its senior advisory board, which includes retired Admiral Elmo R. Zumwalt, former chief of the Navy. An executive vice president of Prescott Bush & Co. also is a director of Asset Management, according to the records.

In addition to Bush's role as an adviser, Asset Management Executive Vice President Stanley B. Scheinman said the President's brother is a paid consultant who helps the firm in Asia, including arranging a recent $5 million investment in the company by a Japanese firm. "He was instrumental in assisting us and introducing us to the Japanese investors," said Scheinman.

Last September, Prescott Bush swung through Asia and Beijing meeting with Chinese officials and potential investment partners. At that time, he told the *Wall Street Journal* that he was representing Asset Management on several projects, including the satellite-linked network inside China. He did not mention then that Asset Management stood to gain from the pending export of satellites to China. He did say, however, that he had not benefited from his brother's position.

"There's no conflict of interest," he said. "This is something that has been going on for years." But he conceded, "It doesn't hurt that my brother is the President of the United States."

Asset Management's joint venture with the Chinese government calls for a computer-based communications network linking 2,246 offices of scientists, physicians, engineers and other professionals within China to the outside world, according to Richard Wall who negotiated the deal. He said existing technology could link many offices within China, but he said a satellite is required for the vital connection to research centers and universities around the world.

Wall said that China has a domestic satellite in space that could handle the outside link, but he acknowledged that the Hughes satellites would offer a better communications link. "The Hughes satellites offer economies and certain efficiencies," Wall said.

Wall and Scheinman acknowledged Asset Management has an indirect involvement with Hughes, which they declined to discuss, that could lead to additional business in China if the satellites are launched. "We are not directly involved, but some people we are working with are discussing needs in communication in China," said Scheinman.

This is not Prescott Bush's only business venture in China that could be affected by an easing of sanctions.

Through his private company, the President's brother is involved in at least two separate ventures in Shanghai. Prescott Bush visited Shanghai and Beijing two or three times a year in the mid-to-late 1980s, the *Los Angeles Times* reported.

Someone placed a telephone call from Washington, D.C., in

October 1988 ordering a savings & loan field regulator in Colorado to wait two months until after Election Day to close the failing Silverado Thrift in Denver where candidate George Bush's son Neil had been a director, the Washington Post reported.

Kermit Mowbray, the former top regional S&L regulator for Colorado, told the House Banking Committee that on telephoned orders from his Washington bosses, he delayed issuing the takeover from Silverado until the day after Bush was elected president. Mowbray testified that field regulators had wanted Silverado seized immediately. He couldn't remember who called him. Federal regulators finally seized Silverado on Dec. 9.

M. Danny Wall, the nation's chief thrift regulator from 1987 to 1989, couldn't recall making such a phone call. Neither could his top aides when questioned by the staff of the House Banking Committee. The call spared the Republicans the political embarrassment of an election-eve shutdown of an S&L tie to the White House.

The financial affairs of the close-knit Bush family is politics mixed with business — commercial and intelligence. Investigations of the business relationships of Neil and Jeb Bush and of the oil-business of George Bush before he went into politics full time in 1966 produce connections to the world of intelligence.

National Thrift News, the bible of the S&L industry, reported in February 1989, in a story curiously ignored by the national media, that a former regulator at the Federal Home Loan Board of Topeka (which had supervisory authority over the Denver thrift where Neil Bush was a director) said "political considerations" kept regulators from scrutinizing Silverado because it involved financial maneuvering with two major donors to the Republican Party.

One of Silverado's big borrowers, Larry Mizel, raised $1 million for the GOP at the 1986 Colorado luncheon attended by President Reagan. Another major borrower, Kenneth Good, contributed $100,000 to President Bush's campaign in 1988. This is the same Kenneth Good who made the younger Bush a

$100,000 "non-repayable" loan.

The retired federal regulator, James Moroney, said that the connections of "politically powerful people" with Silverado led federal examiners to adopt "a different regulatory methodology that amounted to preferential treatment" in allowing questionable loans to go unchallenged.

Intelligence activities surround four of the five major borrowers from Neil Bush's Silverado. Pete Brewton of the *Houston Post*, reported CIA and organized crime links to 22 failed S&Ls. Four of Silverado's largest borrowers had ties to convicted Louisiana organized-crime figure Herman K. Beebe and to an alleged CIA money launderer, both involved in the collapse of numerous Texas S&Ls. Another Silverado borrower was involved in arming the contras and was the business partner of a man who took part in CIA assassination attempts on Fidel Castro's life.

Well-liked and well-connected in Washington, D.C., and Florida, John Ellis "Jeb" Bush has a reputation as a "Mr. Fix-It" inside the Cuban-American community of Miami. The President's bilingual son has business and political ties to members of that community active in CIA-support of the contras. This suggests Bush is tied into a number of people under federal indictment, with Bush himself vulnerable to ethical if not prosecutorial scrutiny.

Jeb, former Dade County (Fla.) Republican Party Chairman and (until his resignation in 1988) the state's Secretary of Commerce, is drawing scrutiny for his "informal" lobbying for Miguel Recarey, Jr., a former high-powered Republican fund-raiser. Political contributions by Recarey and his associates include a $20,000 donation to a George Bush political action committee in 1985-86.

Bush Realty, a partnership between Jeb and Miami entrepreneur Armando Codina, received a $75,000 fee to locate a new corporate headquarters from International Medical Centers, a health maintenance organization that received $1 billion in federal funds before it collapsed in 1987 amid fraud charges.

The company never closed a deal, despite the $75K fee. Bush called federal health officials to steer millions of dollars to the company headed by Miguel Recarey, Jr., a Cuban-American who had business connections to the late mob boss Santo Trafficante, Jr.

Recarey's company, International Medical Centers (IMC) Inc., the nation's largest health maintenance organization (HMO), eventually collapsed, and federal investigators are still trying to figure out what happened to the $1 billion in federal funds the firm received. Recarey fled the country in 1987 amid federal labor-racketeering, bribery and wiretapping charges. An unknown number of Medicare patients were denied services because of the misuse of federal funds.

After the collapse of International Medical Centers, press reports linked the HMO to the contra supply network. Allegations were made that Medicare funds had been diverted from Recarey's operation to the contras, at the expense of elderly Floridians.

Federal officials called such allegations groundless, but it was well known that Jeb Bush was a contra supporter. According to an investigation by the *Wall Street Journal*, contra soldiers were actually treated at IMC medical group facilities. At that time a 50-50 rule limiting Medicare patients went into effect.

Meanwhile, Jeb Bush, had a deal in the works. Jeb had been engaged by Recarey's IMC to relocate its Miami headquarters. Jeb's firm, Bush Realty, stood to collect a quarter of a million dollars.

But IMC was having trouble. Almost from the day it opened, patients, doctors, and hospitals had been complaining that IMC wasn't paying its bills. It was getting bad publicity, including allegations of the company's insolvency.

At the time, Jeb Bush was Dade County Republican Party chairman, not a government official. The Florida G.O.P. had floated his name as a potential congressional candidate, but Jeb said he was more interested in making big bucks. "I'd like to be very wealthy," he said, "and I'll be glad to let you know when I think I've reached my goal...."

At about the same time, Jeb Bush, began doing business with IMC, a $12 million real estate deal.

On August 10, C. McClain Haddow was promoted at the Department of Health and Human Services. He had risen from chief of staff for Utah Senator Orrin Hatch to chief of staff for then HHS secretary Margaret Heckler. Now he had become acting administrator of the Health Care Financing Administration. Sixteen days later, he signed an expansion waiver of the 50-50 rule for Miguel Recarey's IMC.

Two years later, Haddow, testifying at a congressional hearing, said Jeb Bush had called Secretary Heckler to obtain the expansion waiver, that Heckler had approved the waiver, and that she had referred Jeb to Haddow. He also remembered Heckler telling him that she had received "input from the White House and from outside the government" on the waiver decision.

Haddow told Joe Cuomo that Jeb intervened twice, once prior to the initial (and less controversial) waiver, and once prior to the August expansion waiver, each time speaking first to Heckler, then to Haddow. Heckler, according to Haddow, had been "a critic of IMC," but she saw her future in Washington as tied to George Bush.

So when Jeb called, the secretary of HHS did an about-face. She thought "not bucking against the Vice President's son, would enhance her political stock. She confided in me that she believed that she would be a viable vice-presidential contender on a Bush ticket in '88," Haddow said.

Haddow also says that Heckler discussed her talks with Jeb. On each occasion, Jeb contacted Haddow a few days later and "replayed the gist of the conversation consistent with what Heckler had told me." Haddow remembers speaking with Jeb at "some length" concerning the expansion-waiver decision, and hearing Jeb's "reasons why he felt it was important to do this."

Jeb Bush has acknowledged that he did help Recarey, as a personal favor. As to specifics, Bush's son has come down with Reaganitis. Jeb has said that he can't recall speaking with either Haddow or Heckler. Haddow, however, testified that he kept logs of his calls. Jeb has never been asked to testify.

According to the *Journal* report, former Reagan aide Lyn Nofziger (convicted in 1988 in an unrelated illegal lobbying case) and former Reagan presidential campaign manager John Sears received approximately $400,000 and $300,000 respectively in lobbying fees from IMC and other Recarey-owned companies to assist in lobbying.

Recarey also ensured himself some high-powered public-relations help when he retained Black, Manafort and Stone. That firm, which previously employed Bush campaign director Lee Atwater and several other Bush aides, also counts among its clientele the Bahamas and its leader, Lynden Oscar Pindling, who was being investigated for his alleged participation in cocaine trafficking.

After the waiver, IMC grew. Haddow also agreed to have Medicare stop monitoring IMC's progress toward the 50-50 limit. By 1986, IMC became so bloated with elderly enrollees that it was taking in $30 million from medicare every month. Business was booming.

Jeb Bush, by his own admission, never once disclosed his financial ties to IMC. These ties were considerable. According to records released by Bush Realty, Jeb met with executives and representatives of IMC 41 times on their $12 million deal. Once the deal was sealed, Bush Realty stood to gain $250,000.

On his failure to disclose, Jeb has simply said, "If I was asked about it, I would have, of course, told about it." Says Haddow: Obviously, if his father weren't Vice President, Jeb might not have been able to intervene at all. According to Haddow, the reason the secretary of Health and Human Services accepted Jeb's call was "because his name was Bush." It was also the reason she acted on it. Jeb didn't even have to ask. All he had to say was that he was calling for IMC. "I think anybody who understands the Washington power game would know that when the son of the Vice President calls, or makes a statement, he doesn't have to advertise what he wants." Such is the power of the office.

Haddow said Jeb Bush never asked him to change any rules, only that Recarey got a fair hearing on the 50-50 waiver request. Haddow said he made sure he contacted Heckler so she wouldn't be surprised by a call from Vice President Bush. Heckler, he said, asked for a reading on IMC, which he requested from the Health Department's inspector general's office. That reading, he said, raised no concerns about IMC.

Haddow also said he asked his former aide, Kevin Moley, to check IMC because of Jeb Bush's phone calls. Moley, he said, told him the Vice President's office was "very interested in helping IMC if possible." Heckler, he added, told him someone from the White House had contacted her on behalf of IMC.

"She then did a complete turnaround on IMC," he alleged, adding, "Heckler had her sights set on being Bush's vice president, and supported the waiver for IMC on the 50-50 rule."

Moley acknowledged he had received a call from Bush, but confirmed that he was asked only to give Recarey a fair hearing, not to change a policy. He added that Jeb's actions might have been "highly questionable on an ethical basis and showed bad judgment. It was not illegal." Neither Haddow nor Moley says Bush mentioned his financial connection to Recarey, and emphasized that it was not a legal requirement to do so.

Jeb Bush was asked what it's like to be the son of someone in the White House. Jeb compared himself to Ron Reagan, Jr. "There's a fine line," he said, "between using your father to seek personal gain and profit...and just going with the flow."

IMC service providers did not receive proper payment and patients complained of substandard care. After its problems became public, the firm's deteriorating financial condition forced a takeover by the state. Eventually declared insolvent IMC was purchased in 1987 by the giant Louisville-based health group Humana, Inc., for $40 million.

According to Judi Lantz, a spokesperson for HHS, IMC received "nearly $30 million a month in prepaid Medicare payments from 1981-87." The *Wall Street Journal* reported that federal officials were sorting through a whopping $222 million in unpaid IMC billings. Lantz told the *LA Weekly* that the most recent HHS audit of IMC indicated the firm "routinely billed Medicare for unnecessary services."

The audit, she said, also listed nearly "$12 million in over-payments" which HHS would attempt to collect from any Recarey assets which could be seized. Federal investigators estimate that between 1981 and 1986, the HMO bilked the government of some $16 million, $11.9 million of which has never been recovered.

Hired by IMC after he left the Health Department, Haddow received $40,000 in consulting fees before his contract with IMC was terminated.

He was also convicted in an unrelated federal conflict-of-interest case in 1987 and imprisoned. The *Journal* reported that IMC also hired a dozen other department employees after they left HHS. They included Juan del Real, former general counsel at HHS, who joined IMC at a salary of $325,000 and a $40,000 car allowance, and his wife, Claire, a press aide who came on board at $130,000 and a $12,000 car allowance.

In press accounts Jeb Bush was quoted as saying he knew nothing of IMC's problems or any alleged illegal activities by Recarey. He also said he didn't remember calling either Heckler or Haddow, but did acknowledge making "one informal call" to Kevin Moley, another former HHS official, who later worked as a senior advance person for George Bush's campaign in 1988.

Since his parole Haddow returned to the health-care consulting business. He contradicts Jeb Bush's account of his efforts on behalf of IMC, saying, "Both Secretary Heckler and I received calls from Jeb Bush on behalf of Recarey in the fall of 1984." Jeb, he told the *LA Weekly* in 1988, wanted to make sure

"I knew the rumors circulating about Recarey were blown out of proportion, that Recarey had strong community support, and had been a loyal supporter of administration policies."

Recarey was not the only future felon with whom Jeb Bush associated. He was also linked, through Florida party politics and a real-estate deal involving Recarey, to Camilo Padreda, the current Dade County Republican Party Finance Chairman. Padreda, who like Recarey is an avowed anti-communist and contra supporter, was also an influential construction developer in Miami's Cuban-American community.

According to *Newsday*, Padreda is a target of a federal fraud investigation involving millions of dollars in loan guarantees and grants from the federal department of Housing and Urban Development (HUD).

Miami FBI spokesperson Paul Miller acknowledged to the *Weekly* that the agency had cooperated in the HUD investigation of Padreda, but would not confirm or deny any investigation into Padreda's business dealings or association with Recarey, Jeb Bush, or any other lobbyist.

Padreda, was indicted for embezzlement of funds from a Texas savings and loan once partially owned by Democratic vice-presidential nominee Lloyd Bentsen. The indictment, termed a "flawed case," was eventually dropped, reported *Newsday*.

In addition to Padreda, another wheeler-dealer in the Cuban-American financial community, Guillermo Hernandez Cartaya, was indicted in the bank case but never went to trial. Bush and Cartaya moved in the same circles, though no information about the relationship between them has come to light.

Cartaya, a veteran of the Bay of Pigs and a reputed money launderer, was convicted in Florida in 1981 of income tax evasion involving a company called World Finance Corporation. He was a close friend of Padreda.

Former assistant U.S. Attorney R. Jerome Sanford, who headed the investigation into Cartaya's operations in the mid-'70s, told the *Weekly* that he became so frustrated with "foot-dragging by his superiors in the Justice Department and apparent CIA intervention in the case" that he resigned. Sanford says other charges should have been forthcoming, but the investigation was "dropped after I left."

Sanford said he eventually filed a FOIA request for CIA documents relating to WFC. "They came back with a list of documents, but that's it. I never actually saw any, because the request was turned down on national security grounds. I did find out, however, that about a dozen or so World Corp. people worked for the CIA." George Bush was CIA Director at the time the agency intervened.

Colombian coffee magnate Alberto Duque Rodriguez was another of Jeb's business companions who could have stepped out of an episode of "Miami Vice," according to a *Penthouse* article entitled "Family Ties" by Joe Cuomo.

Jeb Bush had tried to free Cuban-American terrorist Juan Bosch, who was released to house arrest from Federal prison in Florida in 1988. Bosch was responsible for a 1980's bombing campaign against Cuban government property abroad, and was the architect of the 1976 mid-air bombing of a Cuban airliner that killed 73.

Bosch received funds for his terrorist activities from the World Finance Corporation, a Florida Company that was the subject of the largest narcotics smuggling investigation of the 1970s. The case was dropped because of CIA interference with the Justice Department on WFC's behalf. During the heyday of WFC's anti-Castro activities, George Bush was Director of the CIA (1976-77).

President Bush's all-out push for extending most-favored nation (MFN) trade status to communist China might be traced to his family interests in that country, and of the role of Israeli arms dealers.

The Bush family is involved in a major housing project in Shanghai, near the airport, to be rented or sold to foreigners doing business in China. The Aoki Corporation, controlled by the Bush family, is the western partner. The President's brother, Prescott Bush, refused to respond to a *Los Angeles Times* inquiry on the subject.

Prescott Bush has also reportedly received $250,000 as a consultant to an American company establishing a communications network in China, Asset Management International Financing and Settlement Ltd. This company arranged for Hughes Aircraft Co., now a subsidiary of General Motors, to export three communication satellites to China. President Bush approved the export of the satellites.

Bush, it should be recalled, headed the first U.S. diplomatic mission to Red China.

Savings & Loans, once meant safety for depositors and dreams for borrowers. It become one of the obscene phrases of our generation. The financial scandal of this century continues to escalate.

Americans forgot about the S&L fiasco for awhile. The Persian Gulf crises took the heat off Neil Bush, the President's son, up to his eyeballs in missing millions from Silverado Bank, one of the worst of the nation's failed savings and loans. It was a complete family affair, George Bush's oldest son, George, Jr., held an interest in an oil well in Bahrain.

While Americans cheered the war, government attorneys were settling the $200 million lawsuit brought against Neil Bush and his fellow officers and directors of Silverado.

By settling out of court for $49 million, much covered by insurance, important evidence and testimony will never be disclosed.

Charming, ambitious and immature, Neil Bush was the personal vehicle used by Denver businessmen.

The forces of greed sucked in Neil Bush. His presence on the board of directors of Silverado was the perfect ploy for the influence peddlers who wooed both political parties and power wherever they needed it.

Silverado's board of directors included a political trophy

whose name repelled the approaches of inquiring of regulators. Neil Bush was in business with Bill Walters and Ken Good, the largest borrowers and defaulters of Silverado money. Both men now say they are broke and can't pay back the money. Walters owes $106 million and Good $37 million. Neil voted to approve all their loans.

Neil told his family and friends that "I sleep soundly at night knowing I live an honest life." Bush appeared before the Office of Thrift Supervision at a hearing in Denver in September 1990. His testimony and courtroom demeanor before the administrative judge didn't do much to foster the "Mr. Perfect" name tag his siblings had given him.

Pete Brewton, the Houston Post reporter who has covered the S&L crisis, links Silverado with nearly 30 other thrifts with possible connections to CIA operatives. He said "Neil came off as a spoiled, petulant brat who apparently thinks the world owes him a wealthy living because of who his father is. He also uses the shtick of being naive and gullible to justify his not abiding by the same rules the rest of us have to."

Dubbed the "S&L Poster Boy" by angry taxpayers, Neil was the child of George and Barbara Bush least likely to stray. Unable to read properly, Neil was tutored by his mother for dyslexia, a relatively common learning disorder.

He went to Tulane University and earned a Master's degree in Business Administration. Neil told the Congressional Banking Committee that he didn't understand all the complicated loan transactions at Silverado.

He claims that no laws were broken and that he had no conflicts of interest when serving on the board of Silverado. Neil's anger at being accused of a conflict of interest and his cavalier attitude regarding his responsibilities sharply contrasts with the remorse Colorado Taxpayers for Justice would like to see. At a protest outside Neil's office at 410 17th St. in Denver's financial district, signs read, "What else lurks under the Bush's?" and "Bank Robbers Go To Jail!"

Mark Stevens, a Denver businessman walking by the protest said, "Neil's a doofus, not a thief. But what the hell is a doofus doing on the board of a major S&L? It's hard to compare a 35-year-old dyslexic yuppie who's trying to climb the social ladder in Denver to guys like Walters and Good. It's clearly a case of mutual prostitution where Neil used Walters and Good and Silverado to further his career and they used him for his name and all the clout and cover that comes with it."

Neil's day in court in 1990 irritated the judge, who several times reprimanded Neil for his loud outbursts. When sparring with the government attorney Neil raised his voice to emphasize his indignance. At one point Neil was scolded for his comment about a question concerning Ken Good, "That's such an outrageous hypothetical, I don't think it's appropriate for me to respond." Neil was told by the judge that it wasn't his place to decide what was appropriate.

While Neil was singing his Silverado stanzas, Sharon Bush was shopping at the new Neiman-Marcus in the Cherry Creek Mall. After a full day of testimony, Neil joined his wife, waved at reporters, and with thumbs up climbed into a chauffeur-driven limousine.

The $200 million lawsuit never made it to trial. Rather than fight the charges of conflict of interest and negligence, the officers and directors of the $1 billion failure settled it out of court, silencing further disclosure. Ed Gray, former chairman of the Federal Home Loan Bank Board, who loudly told a deaf Washington audience of thrift abuse during the 1980s, said, "Neil Bush should be subjected to the same wheels of justice as any other American citizen of our country. The fact that his father is the most powerful man in the western world shouldn't make any difference whatsoever."

Should it make any difference that his father was once the Director of the Central Intelligence Agency and an expert in covert activities?

Was there a conflict on Neil's part? Both Walters and Good

made substantial donations of time and money to George Bush. Walters entertained Bush in his home in the early 1980s, hosting a black-tie Republican fund raiser benefitting the Reagan-Bush ticket. Good flew to Houston to celebrate with the Bush family after the 1988 election.

Before George Bush received the Republican nomination for President, he sent handwritten letters to each of his five children cautioning them to avoid even the appearance of any conflict of interest, no matter what opportunities they might sacrifice.

Jeb Bush spoke for his brothers and his sister Dorothy when he said, "The first thing we can do to help our Dad is not get into any trouble." Marvin Bush added that they should "avoid sleazeballs, people who have quick-fix solutions, people who want you because your name is Bush."

Neil left the board of Silverado a few months before the election saying he didn't want to create a conflict of interest. Neil was aware of the thrift's terminal condition. Three days before Neil resigned, Silverado executives feared a run by depositors and agreed to a consent letter, considered by bankers to be the last rung on the ladder before sudden death.

Regulator Kenneth Mobray, the principal supervisory agent of Silverado, can't recall who called him from Washington instructing him to delay the shutdown of Silverado until four weeks after the presidential election. While in Denver, Mobray was a frequent companion of Walters and Good, who were known to hold their liquor with the best of them.

Neil has said he "didn't break any laws," and that all the loans he voted for "were approved by the regulators." He apparently sees nothing wrong with his proposal of a $900,000 line of credit for Good for a joint oil venture in Argentina with his own company, JNB Exploration. He said Good's lawyer Norman Brownstein drafted the letter and Neil signed it. Neil didn't see anything wrong with failing to inform the board of Silverado that while Good was considering investing $3 million in Neil's oil company, Good was at the same time asking the board to absolve him of $8.5 million in debts.

Neil Bush told the attorney for the Office of Thrift Supervision that he used the "Smith Smell Test" to determine if anyone was using him for his last name, and if he would be offered the same deals if his name were Smith (his wife's maiden name). But his name *was* Bush and he used it whenever he needed to remind people that he was the President's son.

A prominent Denver philanthropist who was an important business contact of Neil phoned him one morning and invited him to a dinner at the home of a mutual friend: "It will only cost you a few thousand and it's for Dad. All the guys from Silverado will be there. You'll really enjoy yourself."

The middle son of successful oilman George Bush wasn't a newcomer to proper political behavior. Neil and his siblings experienced life inside the Beltway and all the social pressure that went with it during George Bush's years in Congress and the CIA. Neil wanted to make it big in the oil business just as his father had. He moved his new bride to Denver to take advantage of the oil boom in 1980. Neil took a job with Amoco. The young Bush couple was embraced by Denver society. Sharon at once formed a partnership with the daughter of Denver Billionaire Marvin Davis, Nancy Davis Zarif. Neil played squash at the Denver Club and Sharon volunteered for Children's Hospital.

The young Bushes, attractive and eager to please, were Denver's political plums, the direct connection to Washington, where politics could provide the medicine Denver's ailing economy needed.

In 1983, Neil left Amoco. His former boss told friends that Neil quit because things weren't moving fast enough. With two associates from Amoco, James Judd and Evans Nash, Neil formed JNB Oil Exploration. Neil invested $100, Judd and Nash invested $50 each. The rest of the initial financing came in a $1.75-million loan from Cherry Creek National Bank and a personal investment of $150,000 from the bank's owner Bill

Walters. Ken Good invested $10,000 and agreed to become the funding partner of JNB.

Neil defended his JNB venture even though it ultimately lost money. A Denver petroleum professional who passed on the JNB opportunity said, "Judd and Nash were snake-oil peddlers who came to me to do some business. I don't know what put me off more, their geology or their suits."

By 1985, JNB drilled several dry holes. That year Michael Wise, chairman of Silverado, asked Neil to join the board of directors. His employees called Wise, "Alfred E. Newman," the name of the smiling face on MAD Magazine.

He was close to Walters, who had mastered the system and convinced many Denverites that he was as unsinkable as Molly Brown. Neil had been doing business with Walters since 1983. By the time Neil was voting on his Silverado loans, Walters was the president of the Greater Denver Chamber of Commerce.

Not everyone in Denver knew Walters' tactics. A former business associate said that he provided prostitutes for out-of-state lenders and frequently sent couriers with payoffs to Aurora city officials in exchange for zoning variances.

Shotgun Willy's, an adult drinking establishment in Denver known for its flashy waitresses, was a favorite of Walters and his "good ol' boys" as they could always count on excellent service including private party rooms in the rear.

Intimates allege Walters was a heavy cocaine user. One of his top executives considered leaving the company as the drug problem began to get out of hand. Drugs and famous people weren't new to the Denver media. *Westword*, a Denver alternative newspaper, reported Neil Bush being referred to as the "godfather" of a drug dealer who kept Neil's photograph among his personal belongings. According to the *Westword* article, Neil let him know when "something was coming down."

Silverado borrower Ken Good was very proud of his relationship with Neil. One of Good's peers recalls him boasting, "Neil just called and I gave him another couple hundred thousand for some of his wells."

Steven Pizzo, co-author of *Inside Job: The Looting of America's Savings and Loans* with Mary Fricker and Paul Muolo, views the Bush-Walters-Good triangle as good business for Walters and Good. "Their theory was definitely 'a Bush in the hand.' If they abuse a financial institution and get the President's son to drive the getaway car, the Feds aren't likely to shoot. Why else would those guys be doing business with someone who poked 30 dry holes?"

Neil's relationships with Denver's fast crowd concerned Colorado Republican Committeeman Jim Nicholson so much that he went to Washington to warn George Bush.

Meanwhile, Neil completed the Silverado conflicts-of-interest disclosure form in June 1986 and didn't disclose his business relationship with Good or Walters. Bush neglected to tell of his annual $120,000 salary from JNB, or of $100,000 that he owed to Walters, who could have put a lien on his business at any time.

Neil admitted to being a go-between for Good and the Silverado board and that Good was his financial backer. He said that although he failed to properly disclose his relationships with Walters and Good, the board was aware they existed as "they were discussed at lunches and other occasions."

The son of a minister, Good was known as the flimflam man when he left Texas and came to Denver. His ownership of water rights on key parcels of land in the Denver area was compared by many real-estate professionals to legal blackmail. Good has 174 trust accounts in Colorado and 45 corporations in Florida.

Ken Good was dynamic, ahead of the times, and diversified in his business acumen. He lived in a $10 million, 24,000-square-foot house. As real estate in Denver began to stagnate, Good expanded to Florida in 1986. He purchased Gulfstream Land and Development in Plantation with borrowed funds.

Good brought Neil Bush and his attorney, Norman Brownstein, to the board of Gulfstream. Bush and Brownstein each collected $100,000 annually for serving. When Good purchased Gulfstream, the responsibilities to provide capital to Neil's oil company passed from Good to Gulfstream. Neil told the Office of Thrift Supervision Court in Denver that Gulfstream had "the opportunity to invest."

The ubiquitous Brownstein of Brownstein, Farber, Hyatt & Madden is known as the consiglieri of Denver's real-estate developers. He represented Good, Walters, Silverado and MDC Holdings, a housing conglomerate with over 70 subsidiaries owned by Larry Mizel. Brownstein served on the board of MDC for several years and resigned last September, in the midst of investigations of alleged wrongdoing, to devote more attention to the practice of law.

Mizel has been an active Republican fund raiser and strong supporter of George Bush. MDC is accused of inflating its worth through phony transactions with Silverado. MDC expanded its holdings considerably in the 1980s with the help of Drexel Burnham Lambert's junk bonds. MDC is the parent company to Richmond Homes of Colorado which sold a $550,000 home to Sharon Bush.

Mizel suffered a brain tumor last year and was too sick to attend the Congressional Banking Committee's investigation of Silverado. However, he attended a luncheon a few weeks later seated with Neil Bush and Ken Good.

Before his luck ran out, Neil's income had risen to $250,000 per year. His JNB salary was $120,000 per year, he received $100,000 for serving on the board of Gulfstream, and says he made "about $30,000 a year" for his duties at Silverado. A sharp drop in income could be one of the reasons the Bushes' neighbor, Fred Vierra, President of United Artists Entertainment (a subsidiary of Telecommunications, Inc.) loaned Sharon $125,000 against the Bush property.

Brownstein is close to the Gouletas family of Chicago, to junk bond king Michael Milken, to Charles Keating of failed Lincoln Savings and Loan and Ken Theygerson of the failed Imperial Savings of California. A former Drexel official said,

"Brownstein was the strong liaison between junk bonds and government."

Brownstein, an acknowledged independent who supports both political parties, is referred to by Senator Edward Kennedy as "the 53rd Senator." Kennedy told reporters in the fall of 1990 that he always stays "with Norm when in Denver."

Brownstein vehemently denies ever subletting office space to Neil Bush or collecting any rent money from him. Carlos Lucero, an attorney from Alamosa, Colorado, who lost the Democratic bid for the U.S. Senate, sent one of his campaign aides to Brownstein's office in 1990. Workmen were feverishly scraping the name Neil Bush off the door of Brownstein's law office in the 410 17th Building as the aide approached.

Bush and Brownstein remained on the board of Gulfstream until February 1990, when Good threw in the towel, more than two years after Silverado had been seized by regulators. Good surrendered title to Gulfstream after the downside of Florida real estate. While riding the short-lived high, one Florida developer recalls seeing Good, "with a drink in his hand all day and a different bimbo on his arm every couple of hours."

Guilt-free Neil told the Office of Thrift Supervision that he didn't see himself competing with Silverado for funds that Good controlled. He said his disclosure and his abstention from voting on Good transactions was "much more than necessary."

Neil doesn't see that his loyalties to Silverado and taxpayers' money could have been compromised when voting loans to Walters and Good. Neil's adamant self-defense doesn't sit well with seasoned Denver businessmen who watched the Silverado story unfold.

Medill Barnes, owner of Straight Creek Company, said the sympathy vote for Neil Bush goes nowhere with him: "The Silverado pirate ship had a willing participant. Neil was no hostage. He was a bona fide card-carrying member of the crew."

It was Silverado's chairman, Mike Wise, who invited Neil to the board. During his tenure at Silverado, Wise was known for his heavy solicitation of loans that required the borrower to obtain more money than needed, then invest in Silverado-preferred stock.

Wise dropped in without an appointment one day and asked Hal Ramsay, the executive partner of Vantex, a division of Vantage of Texas, if he wanted to borrow $50 million. When Wise explained that Ramsay had to pay five points up front, Ramsay burst out laughing and said, "Now, Mike, why in hell would I want to do a foolish thing like that? I've got better rates with my other lenders and I can't see spending all that interest over the years on the five points." He added, "But then, I never took out a loan I didn't intend to pay back."

John Madden, a national developer whose office buildings and art collection are among Denver's most notable, said it would have been easy to be a part of the Silverado syndrome of easy money. "I'm thankful I never fell for it." Madden was stung by Silverado instead. At a breakfast meeting of Denver businessmen, a Silverado-backed apartment renovation was proposed. Madden consented to a $1.5 million line of credit that Silverado could draw on if needed: "Just six months later they cashed my letter of credit. The project was built but not successful. It cost more to put up than it was worth. The developer left town and the project was left without enough income to service the mortgage. I went to Silverado and met with the number-two man and asked him why in hell did he make a crazy loan like that? He looked me straight in the eye and said, 'Because, Mr. Madden, you put up the $1.5 million and we figured you knew what you were doing.' They considered my money an enforcement! It was my fault for not doing my due diligence. It was stupid. If you believe the hype you get hooked. It was pure bullshit."

Money was available in Denver during the mid-1980s from Manufacturer's Hanover bank, Chase Manhattan Bank, Travelers Insurance and several Canadian lending institutions. Ramsay said quality product with good sponsorship could borrow at the normal lending rate at that time which was one half point over prime, with a half-point origination fee. "The only people needing loans from Mike Wise and the Silverado boys were those who had fleas on their projects."

Ken Good says he is broke and working as a commodities broker in New York. He still drives a Maserati and is rumored to have assets in the mountain counties of Colorado and in trust accounts and corporations. He maintains a luxury home in Tampa and an apartment in the Soho section of New York.

Walters has filed for bankruptcy and says although he would like to repay the loans he's defaulted on, he's broke. His wife Jackie and two small children live in a $1.9 million estate in Newport Beach, Calif. He has another home in Palm Springs and ocean-front property in Malibu. Both he and his wife drive Mercedes with Colorado license plates. Last year Walters bought a custom Bentley. Walters says he put many of his assets in Jackie's name before the marriage as part of the pre-nuptial agreement.

Neil Bush and his fellow officers and directors saw Silverado blaze and burn, leaving in its ashes a bad taste in the mouth of taxpayers who will have to pay plenty to put out this fire. But so what? It won't matter to members of the wealthy Bush family, who undoubtedly see this shameful episode in American history as just one more example of business as usual.

CHAPTER 11

And The Beat Goes On

"Excuse me, George Herbert, irregular heart-beating, read-my-lying-lipping, slipping in the polls, do-nothing, deficit-raising, make less money than Millie the White House dog did last year, Quayle-loving, sushi-puking Bush. I don't remember inviting your ass to my show. I don't need you on my show. My ratings are higher than yours."

Talk show host Arsenio Hall

"George Bush, he's on bad drugs, he's sick mentally and physically, if he was a dog he'd be shot. He's a scumbag. That's why he won't be re-elected. He's not morally, physically or mentally fit to be the President."

Christopher Hitchens, columnist for *The Nation*, Washington Editor for *Harpers*, on *CNBC* talk show live with Steve Edwards

As 1992 began to unfold, Texan George Bush should have been riding high. He was president of the world's most powerful country. He was the leader of the Western world.

But he was an emperor with no clothes. As a president, he was an abject failure, a fact that was obvious to many. Even worse, perhaps, his ineptitude had made him a national joke, prime fodder for the late night talk show hosts such as Arsenio Hall whose depiction captured national attention because of its obvious accuracy.

In 1988, when Bush assumed the presidency, he had promised 30 million new jobs. He was about 29 million short, but that was far from the only failed campaign promise.

In 1992, he presided over a national economy in ruins. Foreign policy, once seen as his strong suit, was in disarray. There was no policy.

At some time during his four-year reign, Bush had hoped to glide into re-election on cruise control, presenting himself as the general at the helm of the once-popular Persian Gulf War. That was the strategy his handlers recommended to him: Wrap yourself in a patriotic mantle of a tough, no-nonsense commander.

In typical elitist fashion, the Bush administration was apparently so focused on that image that they did not even see the economic problems that caused so much suffering for millions of Americans. Those very problems came home to haunt Bush.

But 1992 was a troubling time for another reason. It was not a typical election year, when the two parties mount their candidates and hire their spin control doctors to find the right prescription for winning.

This time, the system was turned upside down. The reason was the most popular independent candidate in many years — Ross Perot, whose candidacy at this writing was officially unannounced.

The immediate allure of Perot with the voters, topping Bush in some polls, was bad enough. But even worse, Bush had to be concerned particularly about this opponent because Perot knows a lot about Bush.

Perot had been intimately involved with Presidents Nixon and Reagan in his search for missing Vietnam prisoners of war. In the course of those activities, sources tell us, Perot had access to various secretive acts in which Bush was a participant. So the questions arise: What bombshells will Perot unleash on Bush during the course of the campaign? Or, rather than exposing Bush, will he just drop out and fade into the sunset leaving his supporters in the lurch?

Bush, already facing a defensive campaign in which he will have to explain a lot to the Perot faction, already is looking at a national inquiry into the myriad of intrigues he has concocted.

Indeed, evidence of his misdeeds and his corrupt practices are so widespread that they are no longer recounted only by dedicated reformers. Undoubtedly spurred by accounts such as those told in these pages, even the conventional establishment news media have caught on to the elaborate Bush acts of intrigue.

The latest development, which was unfolding as we went to press, was the perjury indictment of former cabinet member Caspar W. Weinberger in the Iran-contra scandal.

Weinberger's notes, which led to his indictment, are so explicit that they may lead to more charges of other ranking officials.

At press time, Clair George, former top spymaster, was in court facing nine criminal counts of lying and obstructing inquiries into the scandal.

In the latest chapter in the Bush-Noriega saga, at press time, the former Panamanian dictator was sentenced to 40 years in prison for racketeering and drug smuggling. In a three hour speech, he angrily denounced Bush. "Panama was invaded because I was an obstacle to President Bush, who preferred me dead," he said.

Meanwhile, congressional Democrats were calling for another special counsel to investigate what they said were criminal acts by the Bush administration in its policy toward Iraq and particularly in its handling of the BNL affair.

"Such an investigation, at the least, would be embarrassing to the administration," wrote the Wall Street Journal. "It would highlight how the White House aggressively backed Saddam Hussein with taxpayer-financed programs, helping to create the very Iraq military machine the U.S. and its allies had to subdue in the 1991 Gulf War."

The newspaper reported the Atlanta branch of BNL or Banca Nazionale del Lavoro, an Italian-controlled bank, provided $4.5

billion in loans to Iraq between 1986 and August of 1989, some of which helped to build its war machine. The Bush administration has sought to portray the loans as the isolated work of a few BNL officers in Atlanta.

But Rep. Henry Gonzalez, who is heading the BNL investigation, tried to show in a recent speech that the White House had intervened directly in the criminal probe.

The Texas Democrat quoted notes made by a Treasury Department official who had talked with Gail McKenzie, the assistant U.S. attorney handling the BNL case.

One of the notes, which date from Nov. 7, 1989, reads: "McKenzie: She has been called by the White House — got impression concerned about the embarrassment level." This conversation occurred just as the Bush administration was preparing to authorize a $1 billion Commodity Credit Corp. loan for Iraq. BNL itself had earlier provided many U.S. guaranteed CCC loans.

Gonzalez also cited the notes of an administration official that showed the White House — including Bush himself — was directly involved in 1991 in trying to limit the information given to Congress about the administration's policy toward Iraq. Typically, the administration has used executive privilege to limit congressional access to documents dealing with Iraqi policy.

But Gonzalez disclosed a CIA report dated Nov. 6, 1989, that was sent to the State Department and the National Security Council. The report indicated that Iraq was using BNL loans to finance its "clandestine missile and nuclear weapons procurement program." Just two days later, the administration approved $1 billion of Commodity Credit Corp. loans for Iraq, which had trouble raising money elsewhere.

The Journal reported that a probe by a special counsel would likely focus on the alleged doctoring of information relating to exports to Iraq that was provided to Congress by the Commerce Department. "Many congressional Democrats maintain these allegations were designed to mislead Congress and are criminal," said the newspaper.

"Democrats believed that an investigation of the BNL affair by a special counsel would also turn up more incriminating information of the administration's use of taxpayer-financed government programs, or an attempted cover-up by the administration once Iraq became an adversary, or even of interference in the judicial process to prevent information from coming to light," said the newspaper.

In addition to the serious issues of Bush's corruption, effectiveness and direction have been harshly criticized, not from partisan opponents, but from all sides of the political spectrum.

Pulitzer Prize-winning columnist David Broder, for example, castigated the President for his unconvincing mixture of "blue-sky optimism and the scapegoating of Congress."

"The problem, very simply, is that whenever Bush is pushed out of the protective cocoon of the presidency into some kind of direct communication with the American people, the shallowness of his rhetoric and the thinness of his domestic program is exposed."

So much for the emperor with no clothes.

Newspaper columnist David Gergan described Bush's current tenure in the White House as a presidency "on the edge of a cliff." He labeled Bush a "Mexican jumping bean" who traveled too much, gave speeches about nothing, neglected to have any vision and frittered his time away on details. Bush, he charged, knows nothing about being president.

Bush the blueblood has never been in touch with the average American. His stay at the White House has further calloused him from the problems of everyday people.

Washington consultant Lynn Nofziger, a former aide to Ronald Reagan, interviewed in *Newsweek*, said Bush is in serious trouble because "these guys over at the White House don't understand the American people. They never had to worry about a job. As a result, they came at this matter of the economy rather casually." The Bush administration, he charged, viewed the recession as nothing more than another political issue they could dismiss with a catchy slogan.

But continuing unemployment numbers show that Bush remains unable or unwilling to confront America's many problems. Mortimer Zuckerman, Editor-in-Chief of *U.S. News and World Report,* wrote recently that Bush has failed in every way — domestically and in foreign policy.

Bush blames Congress, even though he has no fix-it political agenda of his own. "He says with astonishing transparency, 'I will do what I have to do to be re-elected,'" writes an incredulous Zuckerman. "He gives the impression that his political survival is above the national interest. We have a deficit of $400 billion, soaring costs to service it and a national debt that has quadrupled over the past 12 years, placing a hammerlock on the ability to govern. But all that Bush can say is that violating his pledge on taxes was a mistake because it cost him too much politically. What of the national interest?"

Domestically, Bush distinguished himself by his now laughable "read my lips" pledge not to raise taxes. "The U-turn on the budget added flip-flop-flip to the political lexicon," writes an outraged Zuckerman.

Overall, Bush comes across in Zuckerman's words as a politician "who substitutes campaigning for governing, who used polling instead of judgment, pandering instead of politics, and attacks on Congress instead of real debate. He seems more worried about losing his job than about the fact that millions of Americans have already lost theirs."

Under Bush, Air force One has become a glider. It goes whichever way the wind is blowing.

Are the American people better off than before Bush? No Way.

Author Arthur Frederick Ide writes in "Bush-Quayle" that the supposed gains of Americans have so far allowed "only a few to enjoy the better things in life. The majority of people actually have suffered a reversal of prosperity and plenty —

taking pay cuts, accepting increased work hours, giving up special holidays, holidays and bonuses.

Many of the "new poor" have been pushed out of jobs and homes. But under Bush, his well-to-do friends have prospered. "While the wealthiest families income has skyrocketed 67.3 percent, the income of the average middle class family has dropped 17 percent . . .This means that United States society is experiencing downward mobility and that poverty is rising."

To Ide, the situation is similar to the Great Depression. He compares George Walker Herbert Bush to Herbert Hoover, finding "startling similarities." Both presidents were convinced the "good life" was here and would stay here with little government intervention. They idly and callously stood by while Americans suffered great pain. Banks failed, farms were foreclosed and vast numbers of unemployed Americans stood in bread lines then and now.

As seen in prior pages of this book, Bush has failed miserably at every undertaking. Drugs? As we have documented, the drug trade is going stronger than ever.

Bush's competence even in national defense has been totally discredited. He's the same president who said, as quoted in *Columbia Journalism Review*, that the "Patriot is proof positive that the missile defense works." He made that comment at a February speech at Raytheon's Andover, Mass. plant. Not much later, a congressional committee was showing war footage to illustrate how the Patriots had been highly ineffective.

Bush? The educational president? All hype. Bush? The environmental president who was going to clean up this country? More hype.

Tough on the environment was the "right" or politically correct rhetoric when Bush was running for president. But it's typical of Bush in that his other face was exposed when he had to deliver.

"President Bush saluted that law, the Clean Air Act, and said it would make the 1990's the era for clean air," wrote *The New*

York Times. That was two years ago. There was no election then.

"During the 1988 campaign Mr. Bush often said he wanted to be known as 'the environmental president.' But critics say that while he took strong stands on environmental matters for the first two years of his administration, his approach changed in the midst of the recession."

There's no doubt also that the one area where Bush claimed competence because of his experience as an ambassador has not escaped his general incompetence. That's in foreign policy.

Foreign affairs expert David Ignatius, commenting in *The Washington Post,* admitted that Bush won two wars during his tenure. They were the 40-year-old cold war against the Soviet Union and the 100-hour war against Iraq.

But considering that dictator Saddam is still in office, it's questionable how much Bush accomplished in crushing a tiny country with our immense armed forces. As for the Soviet Union's break-up, it might be argued that Bush was the lucky beneficiary of a timely event. In both events, Bush has typically failed to follow up.

"At the postwar conference table, Bush has been something of a loser," wrote Ignatius. "Instead of acting decisively to shape postwar Russia and Iraq, he has coasted along without a clear policy. In place of careful coalition building that led to the two victories, he has fallen into quarrels with such key allies as Germany, France and Japan."

Then, there was the recent Earth Summit at Rio. The victor of Desert Storm, reporters said, arrived in Rio "isolated and on the defensive." *Newsweek* characterized Bush's appearance there as the "grinch who stole the summit."

Another damning commentary on the President is that he has allowed the U.S. to become the "black knight of the environment" despite the fact that it was America which created an Environmental Protection Agency as early as 1970, long before most countries were involved at all.

In addition, it was in America where a tough clear air bill

was passed 22 years ago and a tougher one in 1990.

Americans spent an estimated $800 billion over the last ten years cleaning up our land, water and air. And yet, under the leadership of President Bush, America, tragically, now is perceived as the black hat.

Why in the world did the American people over several decades allow the Bush family clan to victimize them through its greed-motivated search for raw power and high positions?

The answer is not entirely apparent but it is clear that American history has been fortunate to have produced families of great achievement who passed down their sense of responsibility from generation to generation.

These families have brought honor to themselves while greatly contributing to their nation. They brightened the American dream and for this they will be rightly remembered by historians.

But as this book has shown repeatedly, scandalous intrigues, outright deceptions and downright lying have been the continuing *modi operandi* of the Bush clan.

They have established an unmatched and unprecedented history of self-aggrandizement. They have dimmed the dream of their country. That will be their dubious legacy, not only for those Americans who will later chronicle and expand on these events, but also for those of us who have lived through them.

And where was George:

- When his shipmates were drowning in the plane from which he parachuted to safety.
- When the Bay of Pigs fiasco was planned and executed.
- When the triangle fire teams were put together and trained for an infamous mission in Dallas.
- When President John F. Kennedy was assassinated in Dallas.
- When former Attorney General and candidate for president Robert Kennedy was killed in Los Angeles, after

stating it would take an executive order to open the files of the Warren Commission Report and Records.

- When Martin Luther King was assassinated in Memphis, Tennessee.
- When Ronald Reagan was nearly assassinated in Washington by a known Bush family associate.
- When the deal was made to hold the Iran hostages until the inauguration of Reagan.
- When the Iran-contra deals were being made.
- When the truth about his association with Iraq should have been made clear to the American people.

Don't ask George. He's more acquainted with deniability than telling the truth.

I think we've got a fairly accurate handle on your past, George. Maybe we can make your future as uncomfortable as you have our past.

We'll see in November.